The Practice
of
Being

THE PRACTICE

OF

BEING

Unveiling

Your True Identity

SeanCalvin

The scriptures quotations in this book are either quoted from the KJV Bible
(King James Version) or translated from the original Hebrew or Greek text.

This book was printed in the United States of America.

To order additional copies of this book, contact:
Xlibris Corporation
1-888-795-4274
www.Xlibris.com
Orders@Xlibris.com
Author's email address: seancalvin@live.com
www.thepracticeofbeing.ca
57001

TO JOHN AND FRANCIS,

It is with genuine affection that I dedicate this book to two dear friends whom I fondly address as St. Francisco and St. JohnnyGracekin. This book started out as a personal letter to John and Francis, but as is often the case with my letters, this one turned into an epistle of great length. Sorry, guys, that you had to wait so long to read your mail.

Although it is a great wonder to awaken to the reality of the resurrected Christ in your own heart, it is an experience of equal joy to have the privilege of witnessing Grace accomplish His amazing transformation in the lives of others in whom He is also reincarnating Himself.

The reality of Christ in these two men has not only encouraged me in the pursuit of the kingdom of heaven, but their hunger and thirst for true righteousness has inspired in me a passion to seize that kingdom in the present moment. The truth of the message in this book is substantiated by their lives and through their witness.

Discovering who we really are changes everything. Knowing who we are is the key that unlocks the door into the universal reality of the kingdom of God in our midst.

Thank you, Francis and John, for loving Jesus enough to lay down your own life.

SeanCalvin

CONTENTS

The Awakening

‎———

I t was during one of the darkest nights of my soul when I awoke from my slumber and first stepped into the unseen world. I was not prepared for what the eyes of my heart were opened to behold in the invisible realm of spirit.

It happened one morning just after I had awakened from a fitful night's sleep. Without warning, I found myself in a very strange place. The transition was so abrupt, it completely disoriented me. All my senses instantly went on high alert. Alarm began to reach for my mind. My eyes darted to and fro, rapidly scanning my field of vision for any signs of danger. Looking down I noticed I was standing barefoot on what seemed to be a vast level field, which appeared to have the texture of clouds. *Is this what it is like to die or to lose one's mind?* I wondered.

A slight movement caught my attention. Horrified, I watched as the clouds directly under my feet began to part, revealing an emerald green meadow far below. Before I had any opportunity to adjust to this unnerving development, I began to descend through the opening in the clouds. Strange as it seemed, my descent felt quite natural, as though I was in some type of hovering machine.

As the meadow approached from below, a huge limestone fortress loomed up to meet me. I could not help but notice a horde of mysterious creatures making a frantic dash for the stronghold as I drew near. I watched with great curiosity and utter amazement as they scurried through the large open archway. Once inside, they hastily drew up the drawbridge and immediately scampered up into the ramparts. Their beady eyes met mine at the same moment I descended past the top of the castle walls. Following my descent to the ground, their mocking faces peered down over the parapets, sneering in contempt. Unceasing insults rained down upon me as my feet alighted on the ground below.

Without warning, a hand emerged from my right, holding a parchment on which was written a strange inscription. I read the reference, "2 Corinthians 10:3-5," but I could not imagine what it meant. *How utterly bizarre*, I mused. But even before I could finish pondering what the message might be, a compelling voice, which seemed to permeate everything, spoke through the tumult overhead, saying, "This is your property, clean it up!" As illogical as it seemed at that moment, it came to me that the document represented some kind of title deed for the property I was being shown. I stood spellbound, gazing up at the contorted faces whose voices seemed so familiar, yet never before had I ever seen anything like these extraordinarily distressing creatures. I was beginning to feel a lot like an insect caught in their trap, wanting desperately to escape, when quite unexpectedly and without notice, I found myself sitting in my room again. The shift was so abrupt that I had to shake my head to see if I was really awake. *What was that?* I muttered to myself in disbelief as I snatched up my Bible to look up the reference I had just seen inscribed on the parchment.

Flabbergasted, I read, "The weapons of our warfare are not natural but super-natural, demolishing fortresses, casting down imaginations and every lofty attitude that exalts itself against the knowing of God, and bringing captive every thought to Christ's compliance."[1]

A chill crawled up my spine as it began to dawn on me that the fortress I had just witnessed was my own mind, overrun with fearful and accusing thoughts. I shuddered in disbelief to realize that the thoughts I had seen were not even mine; they had been planted there by the Accuser himself. Until that moment, I had owned every thought that had ever wandered through my mind. In fact, I had gleaned my whole sense of self from the thoughts in my head.

In a terrifying flash of insight, I recognized that I had been taken captive—that my mind was held hostage to a will that was not mine. A sinking feeling of hopelessness began to weigh down upon me as the reality of what I was facing registered within. The life I had been living was not really mine. The identity I had always assumed was not real.

All that day, I walked about in a daze. Thoughts raced through my mind like rush-hour traffic. I walked the razor-thin line between sanity and the world of madness wondering if I could any longer tell the difference. By the time evening arrived, I was literally beside myself with apprehension. I crawled into bed in great trepidation, the haunting voices still wandering through the corridors of my mind. I was certain I would never get to sleep.

I awoke the next morning with a start, utterly amazed that I had slept in the presence of my implacable tormentors. As their voices began to resurface in my mind, fear again began to take hold of my day. I sat up in bed to look out the window. Brilliant sunlight was streaming through the window. *What a welcome reminder that the world outside is still there, as real as ever,* I thought to myself. Then, *wham!* Everything changed.

I couldn't believe my eyes! Just like that, déjà vu! There I was, standing in exactly the same place I had unexpectedly found myself twenty-four hours earlier. Gazing down at my bare feet, I waited for the clouds to open in helpless anticipation of making the same descent to the fortress below. The prospect of "cleaning up my property" terrified me, yet instinctively I knew I would never be free until I dealt with the terrorizing thoughts I had seen the day before. I waited, an ominous foreboding tearing at my heart, the uncertainty of my predicament propelling me to acute levels of vigilance.

But nothing happened. The thick cloud cover on which I stood remained intact, obstructing any possible view of the castle or its inhabitants below. Relieved and somewhat emboldened by the possibility that I might not have to descend, I cautiously began to look around. In spite of all the anxiety surging through me, I couldn't help but notice the amazing brilliance in this place. Warily, I began to turn about, taking in the glorious sights all around me.

Colossal cumulous clouds towered up into the heavens. I was stunned by how breathtaking the view really was at this altitude. I had never observed clouds like these before. They were so dense; they could easily be mistaken for gigantic banks of snow piled up in the sky. I began to take note that each and every cloud was outlined with a radiant silver lining, and many were shot through with gleaming rays of light, which separated into the multicolors of the rainbow as it passed through them.

I turned completely around to observe the massive formation just behind me. My eyes climbed up the steep slopes of this gigantic mountain to its summit, which appeared to be several miles up. Unexpectedly my sight was arrested by a very peculiar spectacle—a cross jutting out of the top of this lofty peak of cloud. All my thoughts bumped into each other as my thinking came to an abrupt halt.

To say the cross was huge would be an understatement. It seemed enormous even at such a great distance. It appeared to be luminous, as though it was the source of the light in this strange place. But the stunning thing about it was that it was architecturally perfect. It gave me the impression that it had been carved out of the solid cloud bank with great care—somewhat like Mt. Rushmore. My initial response was to scoff in amusement as I retorted, "Now who would go to the trouble to do something that ridiculous?"

But even before I was able to finish articulating my disparaging remark, this astonishingly luminous cross began to mutate, as clouds do. It literally began to morph into a different shape—that of a man standing with his arms outstretched on either side, clothed in a brilliant white robe. I watched in stunned silence as this startling transformation took place before my very eyes. He seemed to be the source of all the light I had been admiring. Instinctively and without the slightest reservation, I knew this person was real—more real than I was! In a flood of emotion, all my fears came rushing to the fore, and in utter dismay I cried out, "Lord Jesus, help me!"

What happened next is difficult to say. Whether the Lord Jesus reached for me before or after I cried out remains unclear, but one thing is certain, before I had formed any words at all, Jesus had reached down from His lofty perch, grasped my hand, and raised me up into the highest heavens. There we stood, together, hand in hand, the pure light of His presence permeating my whole being. Time seemed to stop in its tracks. My whole intellectual capacity went on overload. It was all I could do to keep my mind from checking out. I felt like I was very close to burning out a major circuit. All of my attention had become fixated on my hand as I gazed in absolute bewilderment, repeating over and over in my mind, *He actually has a hold of* my *hand!* It was more than my poor mind could absorb. As abruptly as this encounter with the invisible began, it ended. It was as though I fell through a hole in the sky and landed on my bed.

In the splinter of a second, I was back in my room, sitting on my bed. But something was not quite right. I was not alone! Someone still had a hold of my hand. The physical sensation that there was a substantial yet invisible hand holding mine was overwhelming. Fear mushroomed into terror. I was certain I now knew what it was like to lose one's mind. It was obvious that I had crossed over into the world of insanity. As terror worked its way into my control center, another voice began to register in my mind. Quite unmistakably I heard someone say, "Do not fear, for I am with you; do not be dismayed, for I am your God, I will help you, I will uphold you with my righteous right hand."[2] I could not argue the fact that someone was "with me," but who that was, I was not sure. I grabbed my Bible near the bed to look up this well-known scripture.

It was all I could do to focus on anything other than my hand, but when I read the words *right hand,* an ominous dread of evil clenched my soul with an iron clasp. *Oh no!* my fear-filled heart cried. *The devil has me. He's got a hold of my left hand!* Then the crystal clear words

"My righteous right hand" rang again in my hearing. *Aha,* I thought, *His right hand in my left.* "Oh, this is all too technical to be real," I blurted out as my rational mind kicked into overdrive. Yet almost immediately the vice grip that fear held on my heart began to relax, and then it happened again!

In a blink of an eye, I found myself once more high up in the heavens. Jesus was standing perceptibly beside me, still holding my left hand in His right hand. My eyes and all my attention were still riveted to my left hand. It was all too much for my rational mind to process—but then He spoke to me!

However, to say that He spoke to me does not explain what I heard because He did not speak *to* me as one human speaks to another. It was as though He spoke *in* me or *through* me for His voice was everywhere. It was somewhat like having headphones on. It was impossible to detect from where the sound originated. It seemed to be within me. He said simply, "Look at your right hand." It was all I could do to break free of the fixation my mind had on my left hand. I was all but overcome with the irresistible compulsion to remain as I was—mesmerized by the fact that He actually had hold of my hand in a very physical way that stimulated my sense of touch.

Nevertheless I obeyed. I looked at my other hand. And when I looked, I saw something that to this day I have no words to describe. My first impression was that I was holding a sword, but the word *sword* does no justice to what was in my right hand. What I saw had no dimensions whatsoever. To say it was bigger than I was is also completely misleading for I was holding it. Yet at the same time, it was infinitely beyond my whole being.

Then He spoke again, the sound of His voice penetrating everything that existed. He said, "Move your right hand." I smiled in spite of my consternation. "You must be kidding," I snickered. "It's bigger than I am." Yet I knew by the tone of His voice He wasn't offering a suggestion. He intended that I actually wield this weapon. So again, I obeyed. In other words, I let go of my intellectual opinion of the situation and my rational assessment of what was required of me and simply obeyed His word. And when I did, something extraordinarily wonderful happened.

The best way I could describe it is that His hand, which was holding my left hand, was instantaneously inside my right hand. In a blink of an eye, Jesus Himself literally sidestepped into my person, melding His whole being with me, making one person out of two. His immediate, integrated presence made this inconceivable weapon as weightless as a light beam. This instrument in my right hand moved with unimaginable ease, for it seemed to have a life of its own. It was incredible, but I must elaborate on what I mean by incredible.

Wielding this sword was somewhat like flashing the beam of a very powerful searchlight on a foggy night. As with a powerful flashlight, the beam is never longer or shorter than the object to which you direct it. If you point it into the fog, it seems to go forever until it strikes some object. If you point it to the ground, it simply goes to the ground. It was the same with the beam of this sword. It went exactly where I wanted it to go. If I pointed it toward an object in outer space, it would reach it with no difficulty whatsoever. If I wanted to touch my toes, it was not the least bit too long. There was nothing outside of its reach.

However, it was the precision with which this weapon could slice and carve that was most astounding to my reason. I could trim my toenails without the slightest fear of hurting myself. I could just as easily demolish a star in a neighboring galaxy. My filing system of the way the world works had no folder under which to file this amazing experience. It was as though dimensions, as we know them, did not apply to this weapon.

In a flash of insight, it suddenly occurred to me that now would be a perfect opportunity to deal with the menacing fortress I had seen the day before. The change in perspective struck me as most profound. Yesterday I was fearfully looking up at a towering fortress while today I was confidently looking down upon a dwarfed castle. With insatiable delight, I swung this weapon through the castle far below. The energy that was released was indescribable! The power of the light dematerialized everything in its path. At a molecular level, the stronghold disintegrated into oblivion. To my utter amazement, the whole countryside was reduced to a fine dust which was carried away in the breeze!

I became so totally engaged in this task of exterminating my tormentors that I forgot where I was. All of a sudden, I found myself sitting in my room swinging my right hand. I had become so carried away in my desire to see that none of those creatures escaped that I never noticed when I re-entered my room. My Bible was still on my lap, open to the scripture in Isaiah, which I had read moments earlier. I looked at the scripture again, muttering to myself that surely someone was "with me" in a way I never before realized.

As I read further into the same chapter, I was overwhelmed by the words that had been written several thousand years earlier. They described in vivid detail what I had just witnessed moments earlier: "Behold I have made you a new sharp threshing sledge with double edges. You shall thresh the mountains and beat them small. You shall winnow them and the whirlwind shall scatter them and you will rejoice in the Holy One."[3]

Was I hallucinating or was this real? It had never occurred to me until that moment that the words in the Bible actually represented something much more real in a much more substantial realm. I sat there in my room, lost in the wonder of what had just transpired when, *wham!* There I was, back in this place, standing exactly where I had been moments earlier, above the clouds, high in the heavens. The jolt in my consciousness was so disorienting that all my thoughts evaporated.

It took a moment to become reoriented. I collected a few thoughts and looked around, hoping to catch a glimpse of Jesus, but I saw no one. The prospect of being alone in this foreign region did not bring me any comfort. It occurred to me at that point that I had just stirred up a hornet's nest. Having demolished the fortress below, I instinctively sensed that retribution was imminent.

Suddenly there He was, sitting about a hundred yards to my left. I turned immediately to approach Jesus, and as I did, it registered that

He was not sitting on anything—at least anything that I could see. He was just seated, in the heavens. *How bizarre is that?* I reflected to myself as I moved hastily toward Him.

As I came closer, I ducked down beside Him, wanting to get as near to Jesus as possible, to avoid the reprisal that I felt was inevitable. I turned to sit beside Him. The fact that I had no idea what I was going to sit on did not detract from my objective. I sat out of sheer necessity. Compulsively I sat, but as I did, I realized after I had committed myself that I had somehow seriously miscalculated where I was placing myself. In a flash of utter embarrassment, I realized to my great horror that I was going to end up in His lap!

"Oh no!" I blurted out, "I didn't mean—" But before I could finish my outburst of apology, my mind was again stretched beyond all known limits of comprehension. In an instant, I comprehended completely something that had never before entered my mind. For I did not sit on His lap, but *swoosh*! I went straight through His lap and disappeared inside Jesus! It was astounding! I was thunderstruck. My mind came to an abrupt and complete halt. The silence was so intense; the slightest sound would have seemed like an explosion. And then in the midst of the absolute stillness, I heard these words: "And *you* has He raised up and seated in heavenly places *in* Christ Jesus." [4]

Never before in the hearing of that scripture had I ever heard the little word *in*. But now, suddenly this little preposition took on a whole new meaning. *Aha*, I thought out loud. *You mean "in," as in "inside." I get it!* I smiled at the thought of it but then wondered if it was me who smiled or Him.

I closed my eyes and sat there for a long time—although time did not seem to have any application in this place. I just sat there in Him, and He in me, soaking in the reality of corporate being. I was no longer sure who was who, but I knew it was real; and somehow it didn't matter any more that I wasn't sure of a lot of things.

When I opened my eyes, I immediately became aware of a dark, sinister figure standing about fifty yards in front of me, off to my right. I did not need any introduction. I knew instinctively who this was. He was my accuser, whose voice had haunted me internally for most of my life.

I waited for him to speak, but he was speechless. I watched intently as he continued to glare sullenly into the distance. It began to dawn on me that he couldn't see me. He didn't know who I was any longer. I understood in that moment that he could only see Christ and that he could not bear to look upon the man who had so utterly defeated him. In the absence of his accusing voice, I heard these words spoken into the stillness of my innermost being: "There is therefore no condemnation to those who are *in* Christ Jesus." [5]

I closed my eyes to ponder the meaning of these words and more importantly to absorb the reality that these words represented. I sat there in absolute stillness for a moment. Or was it an hour? I couldn't be sure, but when I opened my eyes, I was back in my room—or was I? Something had changed at the core of my being. The question haunting me now was "Exactly who am I?"

What was observed in that moment has taken much longer to apprehend. Although there has been an ongoing outworking of that awakening, which began almost twenty years ago, in that moment my perception of who I had always been was shattered, and my whole identity began to undergo a radical alteration. When my inner eyes were opened to the fact that I was indivisibly one with this infinite person dwelling at the core of my being, I began to understand that His presence was the power of my individual self.

In the true sense of the word, He is my god—that resident Reality from whom I draw my breath and in whom I live and move and have my being. Though utterly foreign to my former sense of self, at a deep level of consciousness I know instinctively that this abiding Presence is inherently my real self, *Christ living in me, as me.* [6]

On that fateful day when the fortress in my mind was reduced to rubble, my whole worldview crashed. My systematic theology disintegrated like the Twin Towers of the World Trade Center on 9/11. Since that event, the thoughts of my mind have come under increasing scrutiny—a scrutiny that takes captive every thought to

Christ's obedience within. I can now understand a little clearer what the apostle Paul meant when he penned the words: "I am crucified together in union with Christ, I no longer live, but Christ lives in me, the life I now live in this body I live by the faith of the Son of God who loves me and gives His life in exchange for mine."[7]

Notes

1   2 Cor. 10:3-5, paraphrase

2   Isa. 41:10

3   Isa. 41:16

4   Eph. 2:6, italics added

5   Rom. 8:1, italics added

6   1 John 4:17

7   Gal. 2:20

Acknowledgments

I am wholly indebted to the person, the presence, and the power of the Holy Spirit of Christ who, throughout my whole life, has persistently and consistently sought to open my inner eyes to the inherent reality of heaven in the present. Although for many years I was completely unconscious of this fact, it has become increasingly apparent that I, like everyone else, have been under the influence of God's indwelling Grace since conception.

I am also deeply grateful for my wife, Lynn, who believed this manuscript could and should be published. Thank you for the tireless hours you contributed to the editing process and the time you spent proofreading this text. Thank you, beloved, for believing in me.

It would be a huge mistake on my part to fail to acknowledge the dear friends in my discussion group who have often encouraged me to put into print the truths that we have shared together over the years: Erika, Jenny, Ted and Robin, Lynette and Richard, Eileen and Rob, Gord and Gail, Dan, Brent and Cindy, Regina, and Norm and Karen. Bless you all for your unrelenting affirmation.

Introduction

What versus Who

We may not always be conscious of it, but one of the most fundamental issues we grapple with as human beings is our identity. We will examine this issue of identity in detail in the following chapters in order to understand better how our identity affects the whole of our life. In order to discover *who* we really are, it will be helpful, as we commence, to clarify the elementary difference between *what* we are and *who* we are. If the distinction between these two aspects of our makeup is not clearly defined, and understood, we will confuse the significant issues surrounding our identity with those of lesser importance. For the sake of simplicity and clarity, we will define *what* we are in terms of our created nature, while *who* we are will be interpreted as our identity. When we neglect to differentiate between *identity* and *nature*, we are not only at a serious disadvantage in discovering our true identity, but we are also severely handicapped when it comes to walking in our full potential as humans.

By *nature*, we are human beings, as distinguished from other earthly beings. Our *identity*, on the other hand, is defined in terms of *what or who we are identified with*. *What or who we identify with gives us our individual sense of self.* For example, when you inquire about a new acquaintance, you do not ask *what* is that. You already know the person is a human being, as opposed to some other creature. Naturally, you would ask *who* is that. In other words, you want to know what, or who, the person is identified with that will enable you to distinguish them as an individual. You are inquiring about the person's identity.

Unfortunately, in our culture, we consistently confuse our identity with the natural roles we play in society. In our respective social orders, we all have identifiable roles such as parent, child, teacher, student, plumber, mayor, etc. Without really knowing why, we habitually identify one another in terms of the roles we play. We equate one another with what we do, with whom and what we know, with what we have, and/or with what we look like. But do the characters we play in the human drama determine *who* we are as individuals? Do these roles actually define us?

For example, if my brother has identified himself with a career in medicine, is the role he plays as a doctor who he really is? What about my neighbor who has a lot of money? Is her identity really "the millionaire next door?" What if my brother retires from his medical practice and my neighbor loses all her money? Do their identities change? Have they become someone else, or is it merely their roles that have changed? What if a famous model sustains serious facial lacerations in a tragic car accident? Is she suddenly someone else now that she is no longer outwardly attractive? Surely not.

Although our natural roles may change, as far as our *nature* is concerned, *what* we are, as human beings, is unalterable. As finite creatures, we can never evolve into infinite beings by nature. The gulf between finite nature, and infinite nature, cannot be bridged—not even by evolution. But *who* we really are is another matter altogether. Our true identity has nothing to do with our human nature, or the roles we play in society, but has to do with our origin—that source from which we have our being. Due to our chronic tendency to confuse *nature* with *identity,* it bears repeating here that we are NOT addressing the issue of our humanity, i.e., our human nature. In contrast, we want to focus primarily on our identity—the source from which we spring.

This subject of identity, which we are about to examine in detail, has to do with our divinity—"the divine nature which we partake of by means of the great and exceedingly precious promises of God."[1] The scripture declares that "we are all offspring of One Father,"[2] which need not surprise us if we recognize God's image in one another. It goes without saying, however, that we humans do not conduct ourselves in a way befitting those who have a divine nature. Something is askew.

Due to a mutation in our spiritual DNA (which we will discuss in later chapters), we are all born with an inverted perception of reality. Because of this inversion, our divinity (our union with God) is veiled under a dominant humanity. Although by original design, our *human nature* was meant to be subordinate to our *divine nature*; our divinity is now held captive by our humanity—by a dictatorial mind. As darkness is transformed in the presence of light, so our humanity is designed to be subjected to the transforming power of our inherent, indwelling divinity. The true significance of *what* we are can only be realized when our human nature is surrendered to *who* we are—to our divinity.

No one can live to his or her potential without an identity. We intuitively seek to be identified with someone or something and inevitably perceive ourselves and others with an identity related to that entity. Our instinctive search for an identity is expressed in the question: who am I? How each of us instinctively answers this question reveals whether we are truly conscious—whether we are aware of our real Self. Do I *know* who I really am, or do I merely *think* I know?

Although some may not be aware of it, there is a profound difference between thinking and knowing! Thinking is something we do with our rational mind, whereas knowing is a function of spirit. The difference between living from our mind, and living from our spirit, could be compared to that of dreaming as opposed to being awake. We would do well, therefore, to ask ourselves where we place our confidence, in our rational thinking or in our inner knowing. Do we live out of our "thinker," or from our "Knower"? Walking through life in our Knower, as opposed to walking in our thinker, is the difference between life and death—abundant life over against the existence of the living dead.

We all have a Knower, for we all *know* at a fundamental level of being. The Knower is our core consciousness—that inmost state of being that knows our thoughts. Scripture refers to this faculty of our being as "spirit." "Who knows the thoughts of man except the spirit that is in him."[3] Spirit is the Knower. Notice the Knower is referred to as "who"—as a person. Spirit knows the thoughts. The Knower is the real Self, that center of consciousness beyond thinking that makes us aware, and discerning, of our thoughts. Spirit is *who* we are. Rational humans is *what* we are. The question is, Are we living life from our *Knower*, or is our life ruled by our thinker? Is our life governed by our humanity or by our divinity? From which faculty of our makeup do we formulate our judgment calls, our thinker or our Knower? Where we place our confidence is naturally where we derive our identity from. "Where your treasure is there also is your heart."[4] Is our identity rooted in our knowing, or our thinking? *Who* we perceive ourselves to be is derived either from our thinker or our Knower.

In the following chapters, we will discuss the distinction between soul and spirit, contrast thinking with knowing, and go on to look at the process by which we are brought to the awareness of who we really are. This process, by which we are transformed from our false identity to our true sense of self, is built into the nature of all things, and therefore is inescapable. However, we can either resist, or surrender to this divinely initiated process. Our choice to resist or surrender is the freedom of our human will. Our response to this awakening process determines the outcome of our whole conscious existence.

Notes

1. 2 Peter 1:4
2. Acts 17:28, Eph. 4:6
3. 1 Cor. 2:11
4. Matt. 6:21

Chapter 1

Soul versus Spirit

It will be helpful at the onset to describe briefly the constitution of the human being. Simply put, a human being is "Being" in a human form. *Being* naturally refers to the indescribable reality of God who cannot be defined in terms of form. *Human*, on the other hand, is a direct reference to form: the form Being takes, which we call man or woman. In a very real sense, man is a hybrid creature, dust infused with Deity—a conscious fusion of the created with the Eternal. Scripture testifies that man, as a living soul, was birthed out of the infinite Being of God: "And God breathed into the material form (the dust of the ground) the breath of lives and *man became a living soul.*"[1] Jesus declared, "God *is* Spirit."[2] Based on these testimonies, it could be said that man as a living soul is the offspring of Spirit Being fused with material form.

It is significant to note that the original Hebrew in the above text indicates that man was birthed with multiple lives at his inception. As an offspring of Deity he inherited the uncreated life of God, while as a creature he *became* a soul life, possessing a biological life. In other words, man not only *has* spirit life, but he *is* a soul life possessing a physical life: three lives which operate as a single integrated consciousness. It is critical to understand at this point that the birth of man as a living soul was *not* brought about by God dispensing life to man apart from His own eternal Being. God does not have life to dispense. Scripture plainly states that "God is life."[3] In other words, man is not a self-sustaining creature. What God did at creation was breathe Himself into man *as* his life, thus making him an utterly dependent creature—utterly dependent on God Himself for his existence. This is significant for it clarifies that the spirit life, which man inherited from his creator Father, was nothing other than God Himself, in him, *as* his life. This fact is clear from many declarations in scripture where *spirit*, *life*, and *breath* are used interchangeably:

- "The Spirit of God has created me, and the breath of the Almighty has given me life."[4]
- "All the while my breath is in me and the spirit of God is in my nostrils."[5]
- "You hide Your face, they are troubled: You take away their breath, they die, and return to their dust. You send forth Your spirit, they are created."[6]
- "If He made His spirit come back to Him, taking His breath unto Himself again all flesh would come to an end together, and man would go back to the dust."[7]

The significant issue here is that man's lives are wholly interdependent. The biological life (man's physical vitality) is conditional upon his soul life being fused with his physical form. The soul life of man is utterly and completely dependent upon the spirit life within being consciously melded with the soul. If the soul life becomes separated from the body life, the body life is suspended, and the material form returns to the dust. Likewise, if the soul life becomes consciously "unplugged" from the spirit, man's soul life necessarily descends into death—a living death. This interdependence indicates that *spirit* is the root of all human existence, the core of all true human awareness. It is imperative that we understand this interdependence, especially when we consider the substitutionary death of Christ in later chapters.

The human soul is a "stereo" creature that stands between two parallel realms: internal and external. As a "dual band receiver", with one face oriented inward and the other tuned outward, the soul functions as a conscious interface between heaven and earth, integrating two conscious streams into a single blended awareness. The outward face of the soul is the seat of the rational mind, that faculty of our humanity by which our inner spirit being makes cognitive contact with the physical realm. Our mind processes our inner knowing in terms of rational thought and thereby creates a cognitive interface between the outward tangible universe and the inward universe of spirit. The inner spirit realm is absolute, unchanging, and without form. The outward universe of material form is merely a shadow of the real inward universe that is formless: "The things which are visible are temporary, that which is in-visible (visible within) is perpetual."[8] The visible universe is a temporal picture—a projection on the wall—of what is absolute and eternal within.

The outward face of the human soul is comprised of three faculties of awareness that operate as an integrated whole. The intellect or reason is the seer of the soul. Whatever the intellect beholds, it appraises in terms of good or bad, right or wrong, pure or evil. These judgments are experienced by the soul as human affections or emotions—emotions that are expressed as wants and desires. These wants or desires (likes or dislikes) of the soul, in turn, give birth to a will. The human will expresses a determination to act upon the desires the soul sees as important, either negative or positive. The unique combination of these integrated faculties of the soul (intellect, emotions, and will) constitute our individual personality. This composite, rational cognizance of the human personality is the outward oriented face of the soul. These three faculties of the soul are what we refer to as the rational mind or "the thinker."

Scripture also refers to another faculty of the soul that is frequently neglected, and thus habitually remains undeveloped. This inward face of the soul is commonly referred to as the heart. The heart is the seat of the conscience – that inner faculty that enables us to perceive in union with another. The Greek Lexicon defines conscience as "the faculty of coperception." Our conscience gives us the ability to see ourselves objectively – to consider ourselves beyond the inherent, egocentric bias of our thinker. However due to a mutation in our spiritual DNA (outlined in chapter 5) we developed a radical deficiency in our inner perception. Because of this inherited deficiency, i.e., this insensitivity of our heart, we naturally depend upon the outward face of the soul (the thinker), which inevitably becomes overdeveloped at the expense of the inward face. The result of this lopsided dependence on external sense is that the inward face (intuition, as it is sometimes called) is rarely exercised to its full capacity of seeing, feeling, and willing. In fact, most of us live our whole lives without ever discovering the vast potential of the heart—our "inner organ of perception."[9] We live in almost total inward blindness (spiritual unconsciousness), our whole existence restricted by and limited to our outward senses. Yet, by design, the human soul was created to walk in a stereo consciousness—a blended awareness of two cosmic realms: material and spiritual.

Within the composite soul, at the deepest center of man's being, dwells the spirit – the Knower. It is written, "The spirit in man searches the thoughts and feelings and *knows* the mind of the Spirit."[10] This Knower is also referred to in scripture as, "the Logos of God who is able to judge the thoughts (of the thinker) and the intentions of the heart and discern between soul and spirit."[11] From birth, this "inner latent capacity" to distinguish between soul and spirit remains undiscovered until the inward face of the soul (the heart) is regenerated. Unless the heart is awakened to this "Discerner" and developed in its capacity to interface with spirit, we default to the thinker which invariably substitutes rational conceptions about reality for the inward spiritual realities themselves. In this fractured state of consciousness, the inward realm of eternal reality is comprehended only in terms of temporal concepts, because the insensitive, undeveloped inward face of the soul (the spiritually dead heart) shrouds our spirit being. This inner shroud veils the spirit realm from the thinker.

Refer to Diagram of Spirit, Soul, and Body in the Glossary

The rational soul, i.e., the thinker, can only conceptualize nonmaterial reality in terms of time/space ideas and abstractions. In contrast, the Knower can appreciate and have intercourse with that which is real substance, that which is formless, beyond the dimensions of time and space. If the Knower within is not recognized as our true Center, our thinker naturally dominates, usurping control over our spirit being. In other words, our created self overpowers and suppresses our uncreated Self. In this fractured awareness, our whole life is governed by our externally oriented mind—a state of awareness that few ever question or consider abnormal. Yet as long as the thinker is unaware of the Knower, the ability to differentiate between soul and spirit is nonexistent.

This inner unconscious state could be compared to being color-blind. The thinker may be able to detect shades and tones but cannot distinguish one color from another. It is like having spiritual cataracts. The soul can see shapes and forms but cannot distinguish real substance from the shadow. Such handicaps only allow a person to comprehend spirituality in terms of religious concepts and/or outward ritual rather than actual encounter and experience within.

The natural consequence of this impairment is that we are oblivious to the rational mind's ingenious power to create a pseudo identity built on concepts rather than on reality itself. By assembling impressive intellectual structures, our rational mind is able to establish and support an undetectable counterfeit concept of self. In this mind matrix, we unconsciously accept a concept of who we are in lieu of who we really are. Confusing the reflection of the light with the light itself, we substitute the shadow for the substance. We assume the rose is red when, in fact, it is the light that is colored. Thus we mistake the "picture" of reality for Reality Himself. In other words, we substitute a pseudo "I am" for our true I AM. We literally assume a false ID in place of who we really are—allowing our created self to supplant our real Self. Even though none of the mental conceptions, which the mind is so predisposed to conceive, could ever be who we really are, we can be fully persuaded that we are what our thoughts imagine. The fact is we are easily convinced that our thinking is one and the same as consciousness.

Imagine for a moment the possibility of simply being conscious beyond your thoughts. That's impossible, you might say. No one can be conscious without thinking! However, if you have never attempted to be present in the moment without thought, how can you be so sure? And even now, if you attempt to *be* without thinking, you will be unable to do so as long as you continue to imagine that your consciousness is based in your thinking. When our essential awareness of self (our identity) is derived from our persistent stream of thoughts, how could we ever exit our thinking? No one can survive without an identity. Whenever we do not know who we really are, we instinctively gravitate toward what seems most reasonable.

But what if consciousness is beyond our thinking? What if we can *be* without our rational thoughts? What if who we think we are is not who we really are? Are you willing to consider the possibility that you are not your thoughts—that you actually exist beyond your thoughts, without your thoughts? If you were simply to "stand behind" your thoughts and observe your thinking, you may be pleasantly surprised to know who you really are! If we would simply listen carefully to the words we use, our words would reveal who the real *I* is? For example, when we say, "I think," have we not by our very words created an ultimate distinction between who we are and our thoughts? Are we not in essence saying, "I (the real self) am processing knowledge in my mind, with my thoughts?" If thinking is something we do with our mind, our thinking cannot be who we are.

It may be necessary at this point for some of us to "buckle our seat belts, because Kansas is going bye-bye."[12] For if we have only ever consented to correct information about reality with our rational mind but never actually surrendered to the possibility that reality is an infinite person within, who alone is able to discern between soul and spirit, how could we possibly know who we are? Although many are unconscious of it, the truth is all of life is sacred due to the inherent presence of Deity dwelling at the core of our being. However, our lives are profane in their expression as long as our soul dominates our spirit, as long as our thinker rules over our Knower.

Notes

1   Gen. 2:7, italics added

2   John 4:24, italics added

3   John 1:1-2, John 14:6

4   Job 33:4

5   Job 27:3

6   Ps. 104:29

7   Job 37:14,15

8   2 Cor. 4:18

9   Heb. 5:14 (Greek text)

10   Rom. 8:27, italics added

11   Heb. 4:12

12   *The Matrix* (the movie)

Chapter 2

Thinking versus Knowing

Many have failed to recognize the essential distinction between rational thought and core consciousness. The reason for this is simple although not always apparent. The majority of us have equated our thinking with consciousness. We have confused thinking with knowing. The truth is most of us have never considered the possibility of consciousness beyond and without thought. We accept Descartes' axiom, "I think, therefore I am," without ever questioning its validity. Without hesitation, we conclude that rational thought is the basis of our consciousness. Never having been awakened to the distinction between soul and spirit, we are not aware that it is possible to "divide between soul and spirit,"[1] and thus we have never learned to distinguish between thinking and knowing.

In order to better understand the capabilities of the mind in regard to establishing our identity, let's do a little exercise. Go to a quiet place where you are alone without any distractions. Sit back in a comfortable position where you can physically relax. Close your eyes and consciously take several deep breaths. Focus all of your awareness on your breathing. As you relax, inwardly take an inner step back from your thoughts and begin to observe your thoughts. Bring your awareness to the stream of thought in the foreground—the tapes and videos that play repetitively in your head. It may take a few moments to transfer your awareness from outward rational thought to inner conscious knowing. If so, keep your attention focused on your breathing until the shift occurs.

Once you are aware of the content of your stream of thinking, review your thoughts in terms of how worthwhile they are. Simply evaluate your thoughts in light of what is truly significant, such as the following: "Finally my brothers, whatever things are true, whatever things are honest, whatever things are just, whatever things are pure, whatever things are lovely, whatever things are of good report; if there be any virtue, and if there be any praise, think on these things."[2]

As you become aware of the content of your thoughts, consider briefly who is doing the evaluating. When you say, "My thoughts are worthwhile" or "My thoughts are trivial," who does the pronoun *my* refer to? Who is the *you*? Are your thoughts evaluating you, or is it you evaluating your thoughts? Are you your thoughts? Are your thoughts you? Is your brain merely multitasking, or is there more than one you? Can your thoughts evaluate your thoughts? Or does this little exercise actually point to the fact that your primary sense of self, that fundamental awareness of being, may not be totally dependent upon your thoughts?

Have you ever seriously considered that who you really are is that conscious state of being that is beyond the flow of your incessant thoughts? Is not the real you the awareness that is observing and making the judgment call on your thoughts? Doesn't this mean your thoughts and you are not one and the same? Is it not possible that you (your real self) exist beyond your own thoughts? The fact that we have the ability to observe our thoughts is sufficient evidence that we are not our thoughts. As we can consider the thoughts of our mind, we, in essence, exist beyond our thinking.

The Psalmist declared, "The LORD knows the thoughts of man, that they are vanity."[3] A parallel scripture states, "The Lord knows the thoughts of the wise, that they are vain."[4] The original word for *vain* is the Greek word *mataios*, which means "empty, profitless, useless and of no purpose." Based on such evidence, would it not seem an even greater folly to base our identity on our thoughts? And yet most of us cannot even imagine an identity beyond our thoughts.

There are some who argue strongly that the enlightened mind is a different matter. They believe that the enlightened mind can be trusted and relied upon. Yet neither experience nor scripture would support such a claim. Have you ever considered the possibility that your own thoughts could be as far removed from reality as the moon is from the earth? It is written, "'For My thoughts are *not* your thoughts,' says the Lord, 'for as the heavens are higher than the earth so are My thoughts higher than your thoughts.'"[5] If God's thoughts are real, where does that place our own thoughts? This universal declaration doesn't exclude anyone but rather indicates that man's rational thinking, in general, isn't what it is presumed to be.

Scripture states, "The natural mind is hostile toward God: for it is not subject to the reality of God, nor can it ever be."[6] This would explain why the scriptures also state emphatically not to trust our own thinking, but rather to lean on God: "Do not lean on *your own understanding* [don't trust your own mind] but in all your ways acknowledge God and He will direct your paths."[7] This is written to the enlightened mind as much as it is to the unenlightened.

The truth is our mind, i.e., our thinker, is completely undependable when it comes to matters of the spiritual realm. It is especially unreliable when it comes to the issue of our identity—which is totally a spiritual matter. Scripture explicitly states that our alienation from God is the result of our own thinking: "And you who were once estranged and enemies *in your mind*."[8] Note that alienation from God takes place in the mind. "Having your understanding darkened, being alienated from the life of God through the ignorance that is in you because of the blindness of your thoughts and feelings."[9] Let's face it, our rational mind, enlightened or otherwise, is incapable of spiritual discernment: "The natural mind cannot grasp the things of the spirit, such things are foolishness."[10]

Yet there are many who consider themselves believers in God—confident in their acquired knowledge about God—who imagine that such proclamations do not apply to their illuminated minds. Their vast repertoire of scriptural learning leads them to believe that, unlike others, they are in the know. However, without the ability to distinguish between soul and spirit, there can be no discernment between what is real and what is merely a mental construct—an intellectual concept of the real.

Spiritual *knowing* stands in stark contrast to rational *thinking*: "That which is conceived and born of the natural *is* natural, that which is conceived and born of spirit *is* spirit."[11] Spirit is that inner place of stillness where knowing exists without the activity of rational thought. Rational thought is the outward expression of inner knowing. It is written, "Be *still* and know that I AM."[12] We only know in the stillness. Such stillness is not merely ceasing from outward activity. It is an inner sanctuary of rest and quiet—a place of no movement, where our thoughts don't disturb or harass our being present in the moment. True knowing takes place in the stillness beyond rational thought. This stillness is the inner state of Being where thinking does not interrupt or dominate our presence: "Whoever dwells in *the secret place* of the Most High abides within the security of the Almighty."[13]

Whether we realize it or not, our core essence—that Center that makes us conscious—does not arise from what we think. Rather, it is this Center that gives birth to our ability to think. Knowing gives rise to thinking. This means our thinking is totally dependent upon our inner knowing for its existence. Whenever the thinker acts independently of inner knowing, it generates a false perception of who we are. In other words, our broken off, independent thinking distorts the reality we live in. It is interesting to note that the ancient Hebrew word translated *iniquity* comes from a root word meaning "to twist or distort to the point of corruption." It is our distorted thinking that separates us from the real world of spirit.

The question that begs asking is why are we so often dominated by our thinker? Why are we ruled by the thought structures of our rational mind—by our biases and prejudices? If we are not our thoughts, why can't we arrest our thoughts when we so choose? If the thoughts in our mind are *our* thoughts—if we are in possession of them—should we not have the ability to put them on hold? Yet why is it that when push comes to shove, many of us find that our thoughts are actually in possession of us? How can our thoughts dictate our lives when our thoughts are supposed to be subservient to us?

Take worry for example. Many of us, from time to time, are prone to anxious thoughts that barge in like squatters refusing to vacate the premises. In fact, very many people are addicted to thoughts of worry and anxiety. The vast number of people on tranquilizers and antidepressants in our culture is proof of this fact, to say nothing of the thousands who are addicted to illegal drugs, alcohol, and other intoxicants. The overwhelming body of evidence indicates that we do not have control of our thoughts, but very often we are controlled, and even terrorized, by our thoughts.

When I first met my wife, Lynn, she was working through a period in her life where she was convinced that she was having a nervous breakdown. At an early age, she had accepted the thought that she would not be able to handle the stresses of life, and like her uncle, she too would become schizophrenic. She did not realize that this thought was a lie that had lodged in her thinking. Her healing began when she was awakened to the reality that her thoughts were not who she was. When she learned to listen to her Knower, she was free to take her unruly thoughts captive. Rather than be ruled by the lie that she had believed, she was able to walk in the truth, free of the insanity that threatened to take over her life. "Those whose minds depend on the Knower are kept in perfect peace, because their confidence is in their Knower."[14] "To depend on the thinker [the mind tied to the outward senses] is death, whereas to depend on the Spirit is life and peace."[15]

How can it be that we so often find ourselves the hapless servants of the ill feelings our relentless thoughts stir up in us toward those who hurt us or speak evil about us? Why do we struggle at times with unforgiving thoughts that arouse feelings of resentment toward others who take advantage of us or ridicule the things that we value? Why are we moved to act in agreement with such negative thoughts and feelings, even when we know in our Knower that such actions are contrary to what we really believe? What is the source of this conflict in our hearts? The truth is, very often our thoughts are in control of us, ruling over us, stirring in us feelings over which we have little or no control in the moment!

Let's be brutally honest with ourselves. How is it possible that "our" thoughts can dictate how we respond? Yet this is invariably the case when we derive our identity from the thoughts of our mind. Whenever we glean our core sense of self from our thoughts, we are not only obligated to listen to our thoughts, but we must unconsciously obey our thoughts as well. When we believe something, we surrender to it. To whatever we surrender, whether consciously or not, we establish the authority of that entity to rule over us: "To whoever or whatever you yield yourself to obey, you become the slave of what you obey."[16] Whether we realize it or not, obedience creates and establishes authority—not the other way round. We are inevitably slaves to that which we choose to surrender. This is an incontrovertible law of our human nature.

The evidence speaks for itself. Thinking and knowing are not functions of the same faculty. The thinker can act independently of the Knower, but it cannot exist apart from spirit being, any more than a storm surge on the surface of the ocean can exist apart from the stillness of the ocean depths. External influences acting upon our soul can move us to think and act in ways that are inconsistent with who we really are at the Center. The truth is our thinking, driven with the winds of adversity, can become a veritable storm within our personality. Yet such thinking is merely the wave action on the surface of that vast ocean of inner consciousness that inhabits the core of our being. This reservoir of spirit knowing is the fountain from which all consciousness springs.

Even though our awareness springs from the Knower within, we live in complete ignorance of this deep inner stillness as long as we are identified with our thinker. The question that is relentlessly being asked is "Who am I?" In other words, is our sense of self derived from the surface action of our thoughts, or is our identity rooted in the infinite depth of inner knowing? Does the passing storm dictate who we are or do we know in our Knower who we are, in spite of the storm? This innermost Knower is the source of all being expressed in all living forms.

Notes

1   Heb. 4:12
2   Phil. 4:8
3   Ps. 94:11
4   1 Cor. 3:20
5   Isa. 55:8,9, italics added
6   Rom. 8:7
7   Prov. 3:5,6, italics added
8   Col. 1:21
9   Eph. 4:18
10 1 Cor. 2:14
11 John 3:6, italics added
12 Ps. 46:10, emphasis added
13 Ps. 91:1, italics added
14 Isa. 26:3, paraphrase
15 Rom. 8:6, paraphrase
16 Rom. 6:16

Chapter 3

Illusion versus Reality

The haunting question before us now is how is it possible that we as a human race could fall prey to the illusion that our intellectual thoughts determine who we are. Why would we believe that our identity is based upon our rational thinking? The reason is simple, yet not readily understood. When we fail to recognize the distinction between soul and spirit (thinking and knowing), we invariably become wholly dependent upon our thinker for our sense of self. This dependence upon our soul-based thinking leaves us lost in our own perception and prejudice, the result being that we unavoidably derive our sense of self from the mental constructs established in the mind.

Whenever our sense of self is derived from our thinking, we unconsciously and unquestioningly believe our thoughts. Without exception, this dependency leaves us addicted to the thoughts of our rational mind. We rely on our thinker to tell us who we are, even when our thoughts have no foundation in the real world of being. Instead of living in the reality of knowing in spirit, we live as prisoners of our own intellect.

A case in point is the apostle Paul. He was convinced in his mind that he was serving God by exterminating the followers of Jesus. Not until his thinking was arrested on the road to Damascus by a revelation of Christ within as Lord [I AM as his true Center] was he liberated from the prison of his own mind. His identity shift was so radical that he came to be known as Paul rather than Saul.

Clearly then, one of the most significant issues any of us can ever consider is that of our identity. Where is our sense of self derived from? If it is merely our thoughts that give us our sense of self, then it is entirely possible that we may need to be awakened to a new awareness of who we really are. In light of the fact that the scriptural meaning of repentance is "to reconsider so as to think differently," we may need to be brought to repentance in regard to our identity. In other words, in order to know who our real self is, we will have to undergo a radical change of mind, i.e., an exchange of minds. Consequently, if we have any desire to discover our true identity, we would do well to examine thoroughly this inner change of mind, which radically transforms everything we behold.

Are you ready to make such a discovery? If so, by simply considering the source of your identity you may find yourself being awakened to the fact that you, the real person, are not the same as your thoughts. Even to become momentarily aware of the fact that our consciousness is beyond our thoughts is to become temporarily conscious, i.e., aware of our true Self. To even fleetingly distinguish between thinking and knowing is to begin to divide between soul and spirit. To be aware of the division between soul and spirit is to become truly conscious—stereo conscious. It is to become present in the moment.

Once this awakening into spirit knowing takes place, we will not be able to shake it. Although we may fall asleep into our thinker again, we will continue to reawaken into this state of inner knowing. Once we step into our Knower, we will never again be satisfied to live in our thinker. Having once awakened into spirit knowing, the dream of the mind-dominated soul will no longer seem as real as it did previously.

When we begin to recognize this distinction between who we really are on one hand and our thoughts about who we are on the other, our identity begins to undergo an amazing paradigm shift. This shift in our awareness of being happens whether we think about it or not. As we become more and more aware of the division between soul and spirit, we find ourselves increasingly identifying with our real Self (our Knower) rather than with the mental conceptions that our mind (our thinker) has formed about our real Self. The more conscious we become of who we really are, the more our identification with thought is exposed as a misconception. As our sense of self becomes more fully identified with inner knowing instead of the rational thoughts of our soul, our allegiance to thinking fades. When our confidence in our own mind is bankrupt, our dependency on the thinker is shattered.

Once our identity becomes fixed in our Knower, our thinker loses its control over our behavior because its domination over our true Self is dissipated. Only then do we begin to step free into our real identity—into our true I AM. As this true Self is revealed in us, we then begin to live life as it was meant to be lived, with our soul subject to our spirit instead of our humanity dominating our divinity. It is by this inner revelation of our true I AM that we discover our true identity.

As has been stated previously, who we really are is the inner knowing at the root of our very existence. Our true identity is consciousness itself, the I AM who gives us the power to observe and make choices. The scripture refers to this one universal consciousness as "the Light of the World,"[1] who "lights every man who comes into the world!"[2] This I AM is the one true Self from whom the whole human race not only has its origin and its sustained existence, but also its true sense of self.[3]

There are many witnesses in scripture to the reality of our common Center—that universal I AM who gives all men life. We will consider more of these in subsequent chapters, but here are a few that bear witness to this Oneness:

- "Since He *Himself* grants to all men life and breath and everything, and has made from *One* all races of men to reside on the face of the whole earth, and has marked out their prearranged and proper times, and set the boundary lines of their situation and condition so that they might search for God, in order, if possible, to discover Him and get to know Him—though He is at *no distance* to any one of us—for *within Him* we all live and move and have our being, and we are all His offspring."[4]
- "He is before all things, and within Him all things consist [have their ability to stand in their exhibited forms]."[5]
- "In Him has always been life and that life has always been the light [the inner consciousness] of men."[6]

When we move over into our true Self, we begin to live in stereo-conscious union with the One, the I AM. This true Center, from whom the human race was consciously broken off when the first man fell into his human ego, is the open door to re-enter lost paradise. The apostle John refers to this entrance in his Gospel account: "This is the true Light who lights every man who comes into the world. He had always been in the world, the world having come into being through Him, but the world did not know Him. He was known to His own but His own *did not receive* [rejected] Him, but as many as *receive* [stop rejecting and take hold of] Him, to them He gives power to become sons and daughters of God, even to those who trust in His person."[7]

To receive Christ in this sense does not mean merely to form a mental conception about Him by intellectually acknowledging the truth of the Gospel narrative about His birth, life, death, and resurrection. It means rather to receive the person Himself as our Center—to identify with I AM as our core consciousness. It involves stepping over into Him as our real self—taking His identity as our own. It means to personally identify with Him—the infinite person within—in His birth, life, death, resurrection, and ascension. It is recognizing that what Jesus Christ did for us in His human form, He did in us—as us! For in all truth, He is our true Self—our core Being.

This is the true meaning of the assertion Jesus made in John's Gospel: "If you abide in *Me*."[8] He does not mean by this that we are merely to adhere to mental conceptions or doctrinal beliefs about Him but that we consciously move over into His person as our Self. The term *abide* refers to a state of conscious awareness—being conscious of Himself as our life. To abide in Him is to live in a stereo-conscious union with Christ as our self—our finite soul surrendered to His infinite Being within. How else could we possibly live as members of His own body except by being conscious of His life as our own, He being our head?

It is this shift in our inmost sense of self that empowers us to become sons and daughters of God. As such we are able to enter the literal reality of the kingdom of heaven. This kingdom is neither here nor there but in the midst, within, inside, here and now! Although to the mind-bound identity such a shift may seem utterly absurd, this awakening into knowing is not an imaginary or contrived state of being. It is the only truly substantial world there is. It is the only permanent abode we as humans have. I AM is the one and only real identity that is available to any one of us—to every one of us!

This in no way implies that the material world of time and space is an illusion. Nor is this to suggest that the physical world does not exist but merely that it is temporary and passing away "like the flower that fades and the grass that withers."[9] The illusion, to which the thinker is so susceptible, is the fallen perception that the outward visible universe is the foundation of reality. The physical universe is merely the *picture on the wall* in comparison to the *real estate* of the universe of spirit. If our perception of reality is rooted in materiality, we cannot help but be deluded; but as scripture proclaims, "Whoever believes into I AM remains forever!"[10] Those that walk in stereo consciousness with the One enter and live in eternal life—a life that has always been and always is, a life that is within.

Based on the external evidence available to our natural senses, our thinker will habitually try to convince us to believe that the physical realm of materiality is the real world, whereas our Knower perceives and discerns that the more substantial universe is inward and "in-visible," i.e., inwardly visible. Depending on whether our thinker dominates our Knower or whether our Knower governs our thinker, we will either live in the grand illusion that reality is materially based, or we will walk in the reality of the kingdom of God, which is the only true substantiality that exists. Living in our thinker is chaos and death while living in our Knower leads to life and rest.[11]

Notes

1   John 8:12

2   John 1:9

3   Col. 1:16-18

4   Acts 17:25-28, italics added

5   Col. 1:17

6   John 1:4

7   John 1:9-12, italics added

8   John 15:4, italics added

9   1 Pet. 1:24

10   John 11:26, paraphrase

11   Rom. 8:6

Chapter 4

The Way to God is I AM

Let's review briefly the ground we've covered. Scripture states that it is the thoughts of our mind that alienate us from God: "And you, who were at one time *alienated* and enemies *in your mind*"[1] and "being *alienated* from the life of God through the *ignorance* that is in you, because of the blindness of your thoughts and feelings."[2] It is evident from these scriptures that it is the unknowing thoughts of our mind that alienate us from the Life who is in us. It is our independent thinker that alienates us from the presence of the One, the I AM who is our life. Our ignorance and blindness are caused by a dominant thinker that has overruled our Knower. In essence, this means that our thoughts about what is real have been substituted for reality itself. In other words, as long as we imagine that we are autonomous beings, our thoughts alienate us from the one and only I AM, the eternal God who has identified Himself as, "I AM *the* I AM and there is no other."[3]

To whatever degree, we derive our sense of self from our own thoughts; to that same degree, we remain ignorant of the one and only true I AM. In whatever measure we maintain an independent identity, we isolate ourselves from the one who is I AM. We remain blind to our true Center, unconscious of who we really are. When our confidence is in our own thinking, we are unable to see beyond the rational concepts of our own mind. We are blinded to the Real by what we perceive—by the darkness that we have imagined is our light.[4] Our sight then becomes our blindness. We cannot know in the true sense of knowing because we are stuck in our thinking—bound by the outer limits of our thoughts. We have substituted thinking for knowing. In this fractured state of awareness, we can never know our true identity because the mind unconsciously defines our identity in terms of what is relative rather than the Absolute.

In this state of spiritual unconsciousness, the mind naturally interprets our identity in terms of social standing. Consequently, we identify one another on the basis of our vocation, our material wealth, our intellectual ability, and/or our physical appearance. This is extremely significant and bears repeating. Because we are restricted merely to concepts about the Real, without any true consciousness of the Real, the building blocks from which our identity is assembled becomes our performance, our possessions, our intellectual knowledge, and/or our physical appearance. In other words, we are limited to mere ideas of the Real, without any actual experience of the Real.

The apostle Paul's experience illustrates this. Before his encounter with Reality on the road to Damascus, Paul was under the illusion that his identity was based on his lineage, his religious performance, his zeal for the law, and his knowledge of the scriptures. Later, after his encounter with Christ on the road to Damascus, he gladly considered all of these parameters as detrimental to realizing his true identity. He considered all his attributes, assets, and achievements as a dead loss, all of which he willingly wrote off in exchange for his real identity—being *in Christ*.[5] He even went so far as to say, "For me to live *is* Christ." [6]

However, if it is true that our thoughts and the perspective of our own mind separate us from the reality of God, we have a real problem. If our mind is the source of our separation from God how are we ever to relate to God? How can we come to God without our mind? The following scripture gives us a clue: "Whoever comes to God must believe that He is."[7] If we edit out all our religious conceptions of what this scripture might mean and simply take the thought at face value, is it not clearly stated here that there is no other approach to God except to believe in His "is-ness." In other words, to adhere to a perspective that there is no time or place where God is not is in fact the way to God. Could we not therefore conclude from this scripture that to consciously abide in the ever-present being of God is the way? This means to live in the *is*, to dwell in the present, or walk in the Now is the one true way to come to God. This interpretation is confirmed by the scripture that states salvation is only found in the Now: "Behold, now is the accepted opportunity; behold, now is the opportunity of salvation."[8]

But how do we take advantage of this "present" opportunity? What does it mean to believe in God's is-ness or to abide in the ever present Now? When the woman at the well in John's gospel asked Jesus how and where to worship God Jesus made it clear that the right approach to God is not an outward form but an inward posture; "The hour comes, and now is, when the true worshippers will worship the Father in spirit and in truth: for the Father seeks such to worship Him."[9] To believe in God's is-ness therefore is not a particular methodology or a specific practice of religious activity. Nor is living in the Now a theoretical course on which we find ourselves in our personal quest for an identity. The way to God is not an *it* but an infinite person who lives at the center of our being.

Jesus said, "I AM the way, the Truth and the Life."[10] It is significant to note that Jesus never said, "I can show you the way." Rather He declared Himself to *be* the way. This declaration to be the exclusive way to God is essentially a claim to be the center of all human existence. In essence it is a claim to be the universal I AM of all mankind—a claim which Jesus reiterated on more than one occasion. When He said, "No man comes to the Father except by Me,"[11] He was unmistakably declaring Himself to be the one universal way to God within all humanity.

Interestingly, in claiming to *be* the universal I AM, is not Jesus presenting Himself as the embodiment of the present moment, the personification of the *is*—the human expression of the eternal Now? Are not the I AM, the *is,* and the Now all one and the same as the present moment? Such claims are compelling evidence that Jesus Christ was intentionally declaring Himself to be the universal entrance into God's presence—the doorway into heaven.

This claim is extraordinarily significant! If Christ's real intent is to present Himself as the I AM who exists at the center of our being, then we must reconsider what we believe about Him. We owe it to ourselves to rethink how we perceive Him. For if Jesus Christ in essence is the I AM, we, as members of the human race, not only have our origin, but our identity from this one I AM. If He is "the light of the world"[12] in a universal sense, He Himself must be the core consciousness of every person! This means Christ Himself is the common center of all humanity.

If so, the person of Jesus Christ and the universal I AM are not two different realities, but one and the same. Jesus is the outward manifest form of the inward universal I AM. If this is true, by the very nature of all things, there could only ever be one such person, just as there could only be one universal way. The idea that there could be more than one universal way is an absurd impossibility. The word *universal* at its root means "turned into one." There can only ever be one universal!

As we reconsider the infinite nature of Christ Jesus, it is helpful to be reminded that our rational soul cannot download the universal. This is to say that the universal I AM cannot interface with rational thought. Trying to download the reality of I AM into our thinker will blow our minds! Jesus addressed this when He said, "You cannot put new wine in old wineskins."[13] Basically this means we can't relate to God with our thinker. We must come to God in spirit, in our Knower. In other words, we can only commune with Deity within our innermost being. Only in our I AM, in the I AM—that core essence that lies at the heart of all human existence—can we interface with the Almighty. That inmost consciousness that exists beyond our rational thoughts and behind our thinking is our one true way to the Father.

Jesus told the woman at the well, "Those who worship God *must* worship in spirit and truth."[14] This clearly indicates the necessity of coming to God in our Knower, not our thinker. To reiterate, knowing is rooted in spirit while thinking is soul-based. Therefore we cannot interact with the universal reality of God with the thoughts of the mind in this place or that. We must meet God in spirit, that core consciousness at the center of our being, which is neither here nor there but the universal presence of One called I AM.

The fact that we can all stand in observation of our thoughts and judge our thinking is evidence that we are conscious beyond the thinking of our rational mind. The question is have we consciously considered what this core essence within us is, which observes our thoughts and considers our thinking. Where exactly are we "standing" when we are analyzing our thinking and judging our thoughts? Who is this Ultimate Observer?

Scripture refers to this universal position of observation as the Logos of God: "The Word [Logos] of God is alive, and full of power, and sharper than any two-edged sword, piercing even to the separation of the soul, the spirit, and the joints and marrow, and is the discerner [the Knower] of the thoughts and intents of the heart. Neither is there any creature that is not revealed in *His* sight: but all things are naked and opened unto the eyes of *Him* with whom we have to do."[15]

In the first chapter of John's Gospel, the apostle introduces "the Logos of God, who existed from the beginning with God and who *is* God."[16] The Greek word *logos* means "universal thought expressed." Later in the same chapter, John identifies this same Logos as the universal consciousness of the world; "He is the Light who lights every man who comes into the world."[17] He then states that this Logos "had always been in the world's populace because the whole world came into being through Him, yet no one knew Him."[18] He goes on to reveal that this universal Light in all men became a man, residing in our midst in observable form; "And the Logos became human, and encamped among us, and we observed Him at close quarters, full of grace and truth."[19] Then John boldly declares that this eternal Logos is none other than Jesus Christ, the one who explains the un-seeable God. "No one can ever see the infinite God, but Jesus the sole heir who exists in the bosom of the Father has declared Him."[20] In other words, Jesus Christ, the Logos of God, is the I AM of the human race. In any case, is it not reasonable to conclude that if we are all naturally capable of observing and judging our own thoughts, every human must have this resident Logos of God, this Ultimate Observer, dwelling at the core of their being?

Yet how is this possible? For if God is good and resides in everyone, why are some so evil? The simple answer is we do not know who we are, and we only imagine we know who God is. In practice we have become alienated from our true Self by our independent thinking. Having thus died to (having become consciously separated from) our Knower, we have taken a substitute identity from the constructs of our rational mind. In our blindness, we think we are ourselves—separated autonomous beings. Yet the truth is we all have a core identity that is one with the Eternal. God, in all His holiness, lives at the core of our being. However, if our perception of self is broken off from conscious oneness with I AM, in practical terms, our soul life can be nothing but a polluted expression of our core essence. The Light from within is distorted as it passes through the "stained glass" of the thinker. This is our disease, which we will discuss further in the next chapter.

Even though our pseudo identity may acknowledge the truth about God's existence, yet it denies the I AM within. For by its very nature, this counterfeit self stands in opposition to the one and only I AM. This means we stand in opposition to all goodness for "there is no good but one, that is God."[21] It is therefore our counterfeit sense of self that gives birth to all evil, by polluting the temple of God with its own religious thoughts.

From where then has the doctrine arisen that supposes that God dwells only in certain people? Such doctrines of exclusivity are merely the blind perceptions generated by the thinker in its attempts to establish itself as judge through religious precepts. These mental conceptions, which the thinker has set up, stand in resistance to and defiance of the Truth, the one true Self. Such independent thoughts not only blind us to the indwelling presence of I AM but generate an incarnate life that is Antichrist—a life that exists in place of Christ. Scripture refers to these rational abstractions as strongholds that need to be dismantled and brought into submission: "Destroying fortresses, casting down imaginations [*logismos* or "conceited reasoning"], and every high thing [*hupsoma* or "lofty attitude"] that exalts itself against the knowing of God, and bringing captive every thought [*noema* or "perception"] to the compliance of Christ [I AM]."[22]

In its self-government, the thinker can only imagine it knows a way to God. The thinker has no true conception of reality unless, and until, it is brought captive to the Knower. As the intellectual strongholds of the mind are brought down and our thinker surrenders to our Knower, we begin to participate in Being. In this experience of Being (living in the Now), we begin to see with clarity that I AM is the universal way to God! We then know, by the very nature of all things, that there could only ever be one way to God, and that way is within—the Christ of God!

Notes

1   Col. 1:21. italics added

2   Eph. 4:18. italics added

3   Isa. 45:6, emphasis added

4   Matt. 6:23

5   Phil. 3:7-9, Gal. 1:13-16, italics added

6   Phil. 1:24, italics added

7   Heb. 11:6, italics added

8   2 Cor. 6:2, italics added

9   John 4:23

10   John 14:6a, emphasis added

11   John 14:6b

12 John 8:12
13 Mark 2:22
14 John 4:24, italics added
15 Heb. 4:12,13, italics added
16 John 1:1, italics added
17 John 1:9
18 John 1:10
19 John 1:14
20 John 1:18
21 Mark 10:18
22 2 Cor. 10:3-5

Chapter 5

Man's Disease

The fact that man has a chronic disorder is a given. The human race contracted a deadly disease at the beginning of history. This disease manifests itself in the insane determination to establish and maintain a separate self—a broken-off, independent identity that claims its own, autonomous right of existence. It is this warp of self determination in man's inner perception that perpetuates all the chaos and suffering in the world. Scripture refers to this distortion in the heart of man as sin. Sin is the matrix that gives birth to all evil.

Although there is a load of religious baggage (condemnation and guilt) associated with the word *sin,* the term still conveys an essential truth. As used in scripture, the literal meaning of the word *sin* as defined in the Greek lexicon is "to miss the mark [the bull's eye] so as not to share the prize." Scripture identifies Christ as "the *end* of the law for righteousness to everyone who believes."[1] The literal meaning of the word *end* here is "the point aimed at as a limit." Jesus Christ, the I AM, is the Center of all human existence. If I AM is the Center of our being, then to miss our true Self is literally to fail in sharing the prize (abundant life)! Consequently to miss Christ as our life is the true meaning of sin.

At a fundamental level, sin is a disease of the soul. This disease is the consequence of a choice, either conscious or unconscious, to allow Satan's nature to manifest through our humanity. Satan, the name given to the fallen angel Lucifer, is the father of all sin. The symptoms of man's disease therefore could be classified by the acronym SIN (Satan's Incarnate Nature). Satan, the first created being to fall into his own created self [his own ego], infected a host of angels as well as the human race with this virus known as sin. According to scripture man's soul (his created personality which is an offspring of Deity), was impregnated by this deadly virus, an infection that mutated his spiritual DNA. This mutation established a foreign identity by radically altering his perception of reality. The nature of man's disease therefore is spiritual at its root.

The disease of sin is communicated by means of a lie. The lie, having been infused into our human psyche, has impregnated us with the conviction that our individuality is founded on separation rather than oneness with the One. Instead of recognizing our union/fusion with the Universal, we live in independence and autonomy. Yet nature all around us teaches us that individuality is based on union, not on separation or independence. By simply considering the vine, we can understand that individuality is not determined by separation from the life of the vine. The individual branches are identified through their union with the common inner life. A branch that is separated from the vine is nothing but firewood. *Separation*, as referred to here, is just another word for death. In our separated mind-set, we are spiritually dead, consciously separated from the One within who is life.

Scripture declares, "Your sin is separating you from your God."[2] In other words, it is the lie of independence, infused into our mind, which separates us from God's presence within. The veil of our false thinking shrouds the Shechinah glory dwelling in the holy of holies at the core of our being. It is little wonder then that scripture instructs us not to live out of our own mind, a modus operandi that is referred to as complete futility: "This I say therefore, and testify in the Lord, that from now on you *do not walk in* the futility of *your own mind*, as other unbelievers walk."[3] This implies that living in our mind, deriving our sense of self from our thoughts, is the root cause of all our futility! The scriptural exhortation "lean not on your own understanding"[4] also reveals our innate tendency to base our identity on the thoughts of our mind.

The question, which begs asking, is why does SIN have such an unbreakable hold on us? How is it that we can be so easily taken captive by this chronic disorder? Is our inherent tendency to opt into our dysfunctional insanity of separation thinking an external enemy? Are we being manipulated from without or from beyond? Indeed not! Our adversary has ingeniously incorporated himself into our identity by impregnating our soul with his own sense of separated "I am-ness." By interweaving his fallen sense of identity into our thoughts, he has revamped our core sense of self. Our enemy has distorted the true concept of who we perceive ourselves to be in the thoughts of our minds without our even being aware of his intrusion. Our real dilemma, as a human race, is that our enemy has become us! By building ingenious fortresses in our minds and raising up mental structures in our thinking, we have been blinded to the truth of our real identity and robbed of our true inheritance. We are deceived into believing that we are what the thoughts of our minds tell us.

These rational edifices and intellectual constructs of separation thinking must be torn down if we are ever to escape the illusionary matrix in which we are held captive. If we are ever to enter the substantial world of spiritual oneness, we must give up our sense of separateness. At the heart of our deception is a false identity. We ourselves have become the enemy without knowing it! Like a virus that hides itself within the DNA of its host, replicating itself in order to carry out its deadly attack, we have become our own worst nemesis. The enemy is now who we *think* we are! In fact, in our false sense of self, we have become so totally identified with our rational thinking that we have now externalized the enemy. Lost in our counterfeit identity, with the real enemy hidden from our conscious awareness, we have come to believe that our problem is someone else, out there.

We have fallen so completely into our own mind that we have become utterly blinded to our one true I AM. Our sense of self is so completely identified with our thoughts that we are unaware of that core consciousness who is our real Self—the one and only I AM—who abides at the center of our existence! When we begin to realize this, we also begin to understand what scripture is referring to when it declares that all are lost. We are not lost in some remote location of inaccessibility. Essentially, we are lost in our sense of self—lost in who we imagine ourselves to be! We have gone astray in our own mind and become lost in our own thoughts. In a very real sense we don't know who we are! Our true identity has been stolen from us, and we are living under an alias, a pseudo ID.

Yet this is not the worst of it. The terrifying thing is we actually think we know who we are! In fact, we are so fully convinced that our fake ID is real that the more we think about it, the more lost we become. In our blindness and deception, we have become worshipers of a false Christ, a replacement I am that is essentially the Antichrist! This is precisely why we need to be found and why we can never find ourselves. Our I AM must come to our rescue! Our one true Self must redeem us—buy us back from slavery to a false god. We must be liberated from captivity to a false I am. Our sense of self must be completely reformatted!

The false identity that we are only ourselves, broken-off, independent, autonomous beings, must be terminated. This concept that we exist in our own right must die! Our imagined selfhood must be crucified. For in this false identity, we are literally "offspring" of the Liar who has incarnated himself into our human souls. No lie can be one with the Truth. True worship of the Father is not only in spirit but in truth![5] This false perception of self, the incarnate nature of Satan, is the virus that has incarcerated the whole world in chains of darkness and death. At the beginning of human history, our ancestors voluntarily surrendered to the lie that they could be as God, having an independent I AM. It was buying into this lie that gouged out their inner eyes, leaving us all congenitally blinded to the reality of "the Treasure hidden within earthen vessels,"[6] the I AM at the core of our humanity. From that point on, our inner blindness as a human race has been perpetuated by our unconscious acquiescence to the incarnate nature of Satan cloaked within our thought structures. Our unconscious agreement with indwelling SIN grants the kingdom of darkness unchallenged control over us.

It is for this reason that our indwelling I AM, our core consciousness, had to be put to death. By "unplugging" the mainframe computer, each and every computer terminal could be logged off, reformatted, and rebooted, free of the resident virus! When the core consciousness of the human race, Jesus Christ, the Light of the world,[7] was extinguished, every human soul was brought to a consequent death. When He was raised from the dead and ascended to glory at the right hand of the Father, the whole human race became a genetic heir of His birth, death, resurrection, and ascension: "For *as* through one man's fault the sentence of death [conscious separation] came upon all men . . . *so also* through the righteousness of One, justification of Life comes upon all men."[8] The correlative conjunctions *as* and *so also* refer to the principle by which life and death are participated in—the natural law of inheritance! We inherit life from Christ [who is called the last Adam] in the same way we inherit death from the first Adam—by the law of genetics.

In order to be reconciled to God, to regain our conscious union with the I AM, our false sense of separate self had to be exposed as a fraud. When our true Self laid down His universal Life, our own independent I am-ness was sentenced to death in union with Him: "If the One died for all, then all died in Him."[9] Mankind's false sense of self received the death penalty. This substitutionary death of Christ, our I AM, ripped open the veil (our inner blindness) that separated our soul from the indwelling glory of God residing at the core of our innermost being. Without the actual death of our universal I AM,

—

our counterfeit sense of being would go on in perpetual blindness due to its inherent instinct to survive at all costs.

Jesus stated clearly that His death would reveal His true identity as the universal I AM: "When you have lifted up the Son of Man [on the cross] then you will *know* that I AM."[10] It is the awareness of who Christ Jesus is that unlocks the prison house of our mind. It is knowing that He is our I AM that sets us free to step into the real world of the universal kingdom of God. If Jesus Christ, our true I AM, had not died, by the very nature of our existence, we could never be reborn into our true identity of conscious oneness with God. His resurrection is our rebirth into the real world of Being: "Except a *kernel* of wheat fall into the ground and die it abides alone, but if it dies it brings forth much fruit."[11] I AM is the kernel of Life at the core of all human existence. This Seed, which lies dormant in the heart of every human, is our one hope of being delivered from SIN. The scriptures refer to this dormant life as "the seed of the woman" who will "bruise the head of the serpent"[12]—the serpent who has incarnated himself within us. It is also referred to as a great "mystery which was hidden for ages and generations, Christ within you the hope of glory."[13]

As stated in the previous scriptures, if our inherent I AM had not become a man (fallen into the dust of human form) and died (on the cross), He would have remained alone at the center of all human beings, lost to us—forever behind the veil of the inner blindness of our thinker. It is a self-evident fact that this seed within all mankind would only need to "fall into the ground and die" once. Nature itself dictates that one germination would suffice for every human and for all time, for He is universally present within all. Thus it is written, "Christ died once for the sin of the world."[14]

In Christ's death, the whole human race actually died in union with Him. We died to the bondage of living in our own mind. But that is not all that took place. When this kernel of life died, His divine nature "germinated" within the soul of mankind, granting the human race the sovereignty to once again choose Life—life abundant. In Christ's resurrection, every person gained the power to live in his or her Knower. In His death and resurrection, all are given the freedom to choose abundant life or living death. The public execution of the human race, in union with Jesus Christ, is therefore our one window of opportunity to be saved from the dungeon of our own mind, that we might bring forth the fruit of God. Jesus made this clear when He declared, "You did not choose Me but I chose you and *ordained* you [Greek *titheme*, laid down your life] that you might *go* [Greek *hupago*, sink out of sight] in order to bear fruit that endures."[15] Ultimately, therefore, death is not our real enemy as the rational mind perceives it. Death, when applied to our false identity (the old man), is a "friend" who brings us into union with God, our true Center.

This is so significant, we must restate it again. If we as a human race had not been put to death in our false sense of self by the death of the universal I AM, there would be no possible way any one of us could ever choose to awaken into the reality of who we really are. *What* we have falsely imagined ourselves to be must give way to *who* we really are, or we will only ever maintain the dream that is created in our mind. In order to awaken, our true I AM must conquer our mind! In Christ's death and resurrection, we receive the power to surrender to our true Self, the one and only I AM. In our false identity, we can only ever determine to maintain the illusion.

This One, inherent within all humanity, is one and the same as "the Light who God has commanded to shine out of the darkness of our own hearts to give us the enlightenment to know the glory of God in the appearance of Jesus Christ."[16] By virtue of His universal, inherent, indwelling presence, He alone is our one hope of recovery from the dread disease of separate self. By the very nature of all things, only an inherent good could overcome our inherent evil. Nothing but Christ in us as a Seed of goodness could ever free us from Satan's Incarnate Nature! I AM is our one and only kinsman redeemer. He is our closest living blood relative! In a very real sense, Jesus Christ is more closely related to every man, woman, and child than they are to their own mothers. As I AM, He alone can ransom us from our separate sense of independent self! Without this inherent indwelling Seed, no human could ever awaken to his or her lost divinity.

Notes

1   Rom. 10:4, italics added
2   Isa. 59:2
3   Eph. 4:17, italics added
4   Prov. 3:5
5   John 4:24
6   2 Cor. 4:7
7   John 8:12
8   Rom. 5:18, italics added
9   2 Cor. 5:15
10 John 8:28, italics added
11 John 12:24, italics added
12 Gen. 3:15
13 Col. 1:27b
14 Rom. 6:10; Heb. 9:27,28
15 John 15:16, italics added
16 2 Cor. 4:6

Chapter 6

The Awakening Birth

It is an astonishing awakening to realize that we, as a human race, have for centuries been living at no distance to God or heaven. The separation we have endured is merely a conscious alienation. We have been alienated from the presence of God by the perception we maintain with the thoughts of our minds. We have been unconscious of this deep inner reality for the simple reason that we are lost in a false identity. In our false sense of separate self, we have had no desire to interface with the existence of the true I AM, who is the core of our conscious existence. We have unconsciously lived in alienation to our real Self, our true identity, because our whole life has been lived in and from our rational mind. In this spiritually unconscious state, our mind has been able to establish a replacement self in denial of who we really are. Thus we live in rejection to the one true I AM!

It was in light of this inner alienation that Jesus challenged Nicodemus, one of the religious leaders of His day, by instructing him: "You *must* be born again [conceived from the beginning] in order to see the Kingdom of heaven."[1] This is to say our sense of self must be rebooted from the beginning. We literally have to be brought back to the original state of conscious union with Oneness, which existed before the virus of SIN took over our human "hard drive." This virus corrupted our inner perception with an artificial intelligence, an illusionary sense of separate being, which is unconscious of its true Center. Lost in the darkness of our spiritual imperceptions, we must be reconceived spiritually in order to see the invisible realm of spirit again. The spirit life that was lost at the beginning of history must be raised up in us again by a birth for as nature teaches us, all life comes from a conception and a birth.

Naturally, in order to be reconciled with Oneness, we must lose our false sense of separateness. If we are to perceive the Universal, we must be reimpregnated with a unified perception, i.e., a single sight: "The light of the body is the eye, if your eye is single your whole life is full of light."[2] In that it was a spiritual death that robbed us of our inner sight; it is only a rebirth of that lost life that could ever restore our inner sight of the Light within.

It is significant to note that Jesus did not end His explanation of the kingdom realities with Nicodemus by saying we merely needed to be reconceived. He went on to imply, "You may well *see* the kingdom once you are conceived from above, but you will *never enter* this kingdom *except* you are *born of water and the spirit*."[3] We must be reconceived and reborn spiritually.

Some Christian traditions give little significance to this "born again" experience. In other branches of Christianity, this reference to rebirth is defined as an all-encompassing event. This teaching instructs its adherents to believe that salvation is secured merely by being "born again" although there is much disagreement on what this term actually means. Because of this belief, many fail to see the reference Jesus made about the subsequent need to be "born of water and born of the Spirit."

There are yet other Christian traditions, which regard Jesus' reference to being born again as one and the same as being "born of water and the spirit." Those who accept this view may claim to have a conception of a heavenly kingdom, but it is only from afar, through the binoculars of the future as it were. Although they believe the kingdom of God is a present reality, they see it as only accessible in the future, at the end of the ages.

Rather than actually entering into the present experience of heaven within, many who say they believe in eternal life have merely consented to rational concepts about heaven. This is due in part to the fact that they have been led to believe that any experience of heaven is attainable only after physical death. However, we are all equally deluded if we imagine that merely consenting to doctrines about spiritual reality will enable us to experience the actual kingdom of heaven here and now, or in the hereafter, for that matter. The truth is, merely agreeing with intellectual ideas about heaven can actually separate us from the reality of heaven in the now. Such mental constructs leave us believing that someday, if we behave ourselves "down here," we'll get to heaven "up there" when we die.

What we often fail to recognize is that the intellect has no capacity to receive (experience) spiritual reality: "The natural mind does not grasp the things of the spirit for spirit realities are ridiculous to natural thought."[4] To the rational mind, heaven is always somewhere else, in another age. Whereas knowing in spirit accesses spirit reality in the Now. Our Knower realizes actual substance in the present moment while our thinker can only conceptualize about reality in another time and place. For example, when we look at the colorful pictures in a restaurant menu, our eyes can entice us to believe that the meals portrayed are excellent cuisine. Yet we will never know whether our belief is true until we put the menu down, order the food, and taste the real thing. The distinction here is between conception and experience.

It is evident that the majority who say they believe in a heavenly life after death have never considered that in a very real sense the kingdom of heaven has already come. Yet Jesus made this fact very clear when He declared, "Most assuredly I say unto you, that there are some of those who are standing here, who will not taste of death, until they have seen the kingdom of God come with power."[5] There would have to be some two thousand year old people on Earth if the kingdom of God has not yet come!

However, the statistics seem to be stacked against the fact that the kingdom of heaven is already here. How many people do you know who are actually walking in an experience of the power of the kingdom of heaven? If the kingdom of heaven is presently here in power, why aren't more of us conscious of this present reality? Although there are a few who encounter the present reality of this kingdom power for brief moments, the majority who call themselves believers have never experienced being in this kingdom on a regular basis. Why is this so?

For many of us, it is because we have been taught to believe that heaven is not open to us until after we die, when our bodies are buried in the ground. But why then would Jesus say that the kingdom of heaven is in our midst, within us, if the kingdom has not yet come? And why did He lead Nicodemus to believe that the kingdom of heaven would be open to him when he was "born of water and the spirit?"[6]

Is it possible that in our mind-bound identity, we have made a serious error in judgment? Although tradition has taken Jesus' statement about being "born of water and the spirit" to be one and the same as being born again, there is sufficient evidence to consider that one is as different from, and subsequent to, the other, as being born out of the womb is distinct from, and secondary to, being conceived in the womb.

It is interesting to note that the word *born*, which Jesus uses in His consultation with Nicodemus, is the same Greek word *gennao* that occurs in Matthew's Gospel where it speaks of Jesus being conceived in Mary's womb by the Holy Spirit: "For that which is *conceived within her* [*gennao*] is of the Holy Spirit."[7] The Greek word *gennao* by definition means "to procreate," (properly of the father, but by extension of the mother). Figuratively, it means "to regenerate, bear, beget, be born, bring forth, conceive, be delivered of, gender, make, spring."[8]

Consider for a moment the implications of this definition. Where does it lead us? Could it be that many of those who claim they are "saved" are merely "conceived in the womb," only imagining that they are born "out of the womb." If we are meant to be walking in the experience of the kingdom of heaven now, can it be said that we are saved, in the true sense of the word, if we have never yet entered the real world? Although you may find it very disturbing, this misconception is entirely possible due to the fact that for centuries, the consensus in most branches of Christian tradition is that heaven is only accessible after death. Add to that the fact that many have been taught that if one is simply born again (conceived in the womb), they have realized everything there is to experience in the present moment.

But what if heaven *is* accessible now, here on earth? Maybe we need to seriously reconsider what Jesus said about heaven being here and now. Putting off our entrance into the kingdom of heaven until a later time could have significant consequences. It could be likened to one unborn fetus sharing his conceptions about the world beyond the womb with his fraternal twin in the womb, saying, "We have new life, so we must be experiencing all there is." Such a conception may be true in the sense that the twins are experiencing all they can at that precise moment. Yet if they were to "set up house" in the womb on the basis of their present experience, it would be a great tragedy. It would be a denial of their true potential as human beings! The same could be said about those who miss their present-tense entrance into the kingdom of heaven since this entrance has been promised in the here and now!

Have you seriously considered the reality of what Jesus revealed about the kingdom of heaven? Is it not possible that the kingdom of heaven is literally in our midst—within us, even though a great number (possibly the majority) have never yet been birthed (*gennao*) into this kingdom of heaven? If being born again is only a conception, a germination of the spirit of I AM within our inner being that brings about a fusion of God's divine nature with our humanity, then many who claim to be saved may still need to be born into the real world by a subsequent baptism in the Spirit. It is quite possible that many have only experienced a conception of the kingdom of heaven (an inner sight of the kingdom) without ever having been delivered into it by being "born of water and the spirit."

According to Jesus' teaching, our awakening to the kingdom of heaven requires an "in-birth," a conception of Christ in our hearts. Whereas our entrance into the kingdom requires an "out-birth," i.e., being "delivered from the power of darkness and translated into the kingdom of Light."[9]

Notes

1   John 3:3-5, italics added
2   Matt. 6:22
3   John 3:5, italics added
4   1 Cor. 2:14, paraphrase
5   Mark 9:1
6   John 3:5
7   Matt. 1:20, italics added
8   Strong's Concordance
9   Col. 1:13

Chapter 7

Where Is Heaven?

Has it ever crossed your mind that there may be an entrance into heaven awaiting you in this moment? Are you willing to consider that heaven may be a much more immanent reality than you have ever imagined? Are you open to the possibility that you may even have resisted entering into this kingdom in the present moment due to an addiction to your own "religious" thoughts about heaven?

In our familiarity with rational concepts about heaven, we are often hesitant to leave the "womb" of our mind. In fact, many of us are actually terrified to give up our doctrinal assumptions about heaven in order to enter and be in that kingdom here and now. We are like the little tree that sprouted in the greenhouse that now doesn't want to leave the security and comfort of indoors to be planted out in the universe.

Jesus announced that the kingdom of God had come. He also declared that "the kingdom of heaven is near, at hand."[1] In other words, this kingdom is here, presently within us now. In light of these pronouncements, it is only reasonable to conclude that we are meant to be living in the reality of the kingdom of heaven before we leave this material realm, before we exit our mortal bodies. If this is true, what has hindered us from entering into the present reality of this kingdom in our midst, except our mistaken beliefs about heaven and its accessibility? In other words, our perception and our thinking could very easily separate us from the present experience of heaven!

The reason many of us have never gained access to this kingdom is because we've unconsciously "clung to the walls of the womb" in a desperate attempt to maintain our rational conceptions about heaven. We have merely related to one another with mental constructs (ideas and concepts) about the kingdom of heaven, when by now we could have been walking in this kingdom experientially. As long as we walk in our thinker, we automatically substitute our doctrinal beliefs about heaven for the reality of heaven itself. It is only natural therefore that we default to the assumption that conceptualization about heaven is as real as it gets for now.

In his conversation with Nicodemus, Jesus makes it abundantly clear that the kingdom of heaven will become perceivable to those who are "born from the beginning" (conceived from above). However, he goes further by declaring that there is also available an actual entrance into the kingdom of heaven here and now. In order to perceive and enter this kingdom, Jesus describes two experiential prerequisites. First, we must be born from the beginning, and second, we must be born of water and the spirit: "Truly, truly, I explain to you, except a person is conceived from the beginning, he *cannot see* the kingdom of God. Most assuredly, I declare to you, except a person is born of water and the Spirit, he *cannot enter* into the kingdom of God."[2]

Briefly consider this latter statement of Jesus outside of any religious context in which you may have heard it previously. Ponder Jesus' words here in the context of the following directives offered to a viable unborn fetus: "You cannot enter the world at large until you let go of your life in the womb. Unless you exit the birth canal and start breathing air, you cannot participate in life on planet Earth."

This is to say, there are certain developmental requirements that must take place before a fetus is capable of participating in life beyond the womb. As surely as the fetus must "let go" of the umbilical cord in order to join the world at large, even so we also must let go of our former perceptions of reality in order to enter the real world of spirit. Our fundamentally immature sense of self must give way to our true identity before we can enter the kingdom of heaven. We must "put off the old man with his practices and put on the new self who is renewed in the spirit of knowing."[3] Unless we let go of our mind-bound identity, come out of our thinker, and move over into our Knower, we cannot enter the kingdom of heaven!

If these considerations are valid, what was Jesus referring to when He said, "You *must* be '*gennao*' of water and the Spirit in order to participate in this 'inner kingdom'"?[4] In other words, if we not only have to be spiritually conceived but also delivered (birthed) by a spiritual baptism in order to participate in the kingdom of heaven, what does our actual "delivery" involve?

In Matthew's Gospel, John the Baptizer makes a statement that initially may seem completely unrelated to this birthing process, which Jesus spoke of to Nicodemus. Yet if we are willing to look beyond where our religious conditioning has taken us, we will recognize at least a vague familiarity to the subject being discussed. John cautions his disciples: "I indeed *baptize you with water* unto repentance: but He who comes after me is mightier than I, whose shoes I am not worthy to loosen; He shall *baptize you with the Holy Spirit*, and with fire. Whose fan is in His hand, and He will thoroughly purge His floor, and gather His wheat into the granary; but He will burn up the chaff with unquenchable fire."[5]

Is it possible that Jesus' revelation to Nicodemus about being "born of water" has a direct correlation to John's water baptism of repentance while being "born of the Spirit" corresponds expressly to being "baptized with the Holy Spirit and with fire"? In other words, does this baptism, which John speaks of, have anything to do with the birth that Jesus said is required to enter into the kingdom of heaven? Are these two events related, and if so, how? Matthew's account of Jesus' baptism gives us more clues.

Then Jesus came from Galilee to the Jordan, to be baptized by John. But John utterly forbid Him, saying, "I have need to be baptized by You. How is it that You come to me?" And Jesus answered him, "Let it be so now, for in this way we will properly fulfill all righteousness." Then he yielded to Him. And *when Jesus was baptized, He immediately went up out of the water: and, lo, the heavens were opened unto Him,* and *He saw* the Spirit of God descending like a dove, lighting upon Him: And behold [He heard], a voice from heaven, saying, "This is my beloved Son, in whom I am well pleased."[6]

This same account is also recorded in Mark's Gospel:

And it came to pass in those days that Jesus came from Nazareth of Galilee, and *He was baptized by John in the Jordan. And straightway coming up out of the water, He saw the heavens opened,* and the Spirit, like a dove, descending upon Him. And there came a voice from heaven, saying, "You are my beloved Son, in whom I am well pleased." And immediately the Spirit drove Him into the wilderness. And He was there in the wilderness forty days, tempted of Satan; and was with the wild beasts; and the angels ministered unto Him.[7]

The statement, "when Jesus was baptized, He immediately went up out of the water: and, behold, the heavens were opened unto Him"[8] describes a scenario that is noticeably parallel to what Jesus told Nicodemus in John 3. As with Jesus' baptism by John (a water baptism unto repentance, which endowed Jesus with the Spirit), our entrance into the kingdom of heaven is opened to us in like manner. In other words, upon our spiritual baptism of repentance by the Spirit (our being "born of water and the Spirit"[9]), we gain access to the kingdom of heaven. Is it not explicitly stated in both accounts that when Jesus was baptized with water and the Spirit, He immediately had access to heaven? Is this merely a coincidence, or is the evidence pointing to the same entrance into the kingdom of heaven, which Jesus spoke of to Nicodemus?

This entrance does not grant us access to an outwardly visible kingdom but rather a much more real kingdom within our hearts: "And when the Pharisees put questions to Him about when the kingdom of God would come, He answered them saying: 'The kingdom of God will not come through visual observation, and men will not say: "See, it is here!" or, "There!" For the kingdom of God is within you.'"[10]

This kingdom of heaven could be illustrated in terms of the Internet, the global system of computer networks. Like the kingdom of heaven, the Internet cannot be described in terms of here or there because it is a universal phenomenon. Although it has no outwardly observable address, the Internet is a real "place." It is a network of networks within cyberspace. As with the kingdom of heaven, the Internet has a door. This door (point of access) is known as an IP (Internet protocol) address. The Internet is accessible only from within a computer that is configured with this IP. In like manner, the kingdom of heaven can only be accessed from within the heart of man, according to a prescribed protocol.

As with the Internet, these kingdom protocols must be strictly adhered to if one is to gain access to this inner universal reality of God. Jesus announced these kingdom protocols in many of His parables. Here are a few examples:

- "Truly I say unto you, Whosoever shall not receive the kingdom of God as a little child shall in no wise enter therein."[11]
- "Most assuredly I say unto you, Except you are converted [turn self about], and become as little children, you cannot enter into the kingdom of heaven."[12]

- "Except your righteousness shall exceed the righteousness of the scribes and Pharisees [pastors and religious teachers], you shall in no case enter into the kingdom of heaven."[13]
- "Children, how hard is it for them that trust in riches to enter into the kingdom of God!"[14]
- "Truly, truly I say unto you, except a person is born of water and of the Spirit, he cannot enter into the kingdom of God."[15]

As radical as this may be for us to consider, is it not possible that heaven is at no distance to anyone right now? Like the Internet, is not heaven in the same room we are? Are you willing to consider that this entrance into the kingdom of heaven is open to you, in the inner realm of spirit, at this very moment? According to what Jesus said and as verified by His own experience, the evidence indicates that heaven is accessible here—in the now.

Notes

1   Matt. 4:17
2   John 3:5,6, italics added
3   Col 3:9,10, Eph. 4:22,23
4   John 3:5,6, paraphrase
5   Matt. 3:11, italics added
6   Matt. 3:13-17, italics added
7   Mark 1:9-13, italics added
8   Mark 1:10
9   John 3:5
10   Luke 17:21
11   Luke 18:17
12   Matt. 18:3
13   Matt. 5:20
14   Mark 10:24
15   John 3:5

Chapter 8

Did Jesus Have to Repent?

For some, there may appear to be a discrepancy with the interpretation that heaven is opened to us in the same way it was opened to Jesus at his baptism. The obvious question that arises is why would Jesus have to undergo a baptism of repentance? If He was "without sin,"[1] as the scriptures declare, what would Jesus have to repent for?

Recall briefly how John responded when Jesus requested that he baptize Him. His adamant refusal to baptize Jesus was overruled by Christ's resolute declaration: "It is necessary we do this in order to properly fulfill all righteousness."[2] This revelation indicates that it was, in fact, required that Jesus undergo this water baptism of repentance in order to enter the kingdom of heaven on earth. In light of the fact that Jesus had to "learn obedience,"[3] what is the underlying significance of this baptism of repentance John was called to perform?

If our understanding of repentance is limited to traditional thought, we most likely will not have recognized what true repentance is. In other words, we may not have considered Jesus' baptism in terms of what was required of Him to access the kingdom of heaven on earth. Clearly, Jesus' baptism by John has little to do with our traditional view of repentance, or, for that matter, with our traditional view of baptism. Most interpret baptism to be an outward witness of salvation while, traditionally, repentance has come to be defined as "feelings of remorse that move us to ask for forgiveness for our failures, with a renewed commitment to do better next time." This definition describes the "godly sorrow which leads to repentance,"[4] but it does not define the repentance to which Jesus and John referred. As used in the third chapter of John's Gospel, the verb to repent literally means "to reconsider so as to think differently."[5] Repentance therefore is simply a change of mind.

How then does a baptism of repentance prepare the way for humans to enter the kingdom of heaven? In what sense did Jesus have to repent [reconsider] in order for heaven to be opened to Him? In other words, what is the real significance of Jesus' baptism by John in regard to His mind-set? Clearly Jesus had no need to be born again, conceived from above, for scripture clearly declares that He was conceived of the Spirit in Mary's womb: "The Holy Spirit shall come in upon you, and the miraculous ability of the Most High shall endow you with supernatural power: therefore also that holy one which shall be born of you shall be called the Son of God."[6]

It would seem however from what Jesus told Nicodemus and from what transpired at His baptism that He did need to be "born of water and the Spirit." If repentance is a change of mind (or more correctly, an exchange of mind), Jesus must have had to repent, in the true sense of the word, in order to enter and walk in the kingdom of heaven on earth. Otherwise He would not have said it was necessary that He be baptized with this baptism of repentance.

Look again at the beginning of Mark's Gospel and consider carefully what took place immediately following Jesus' baptism. When Jesus was "born of water and the Spirit," what is the first thing the Spirit compels Jesus to do? What happened directly after heaven was opened to Him? "And immediately the Spirit cast Him into the wilderness. And He was there in the wilderness forty days, tempted of Satan; and was with the wild beasts, and the angels ministered unto Him."[7]

It is interesting to note that the verb *to cast*, which is used to describe the Spirit's activity, is the Greek word *ekballo*, which literally means "to eject or to cast out."[8] It is the same word used by Mark where he recorded that Jesus "preached in their synagogues throughout all Galilee, and cast out [*ekballo*] devils."[9] The next question is why would the endowment of the Holy Spirit, which came upon Jesus at His baptism, literally throw Him out into the wilderness with the wild beasts for forty days to be tested by the devil and enticed to sin? Somehow this doesn't seem like a very "holy" baptism. Did not Jesus explicitly instruct His disciples to pray that the Father would not lead them into temptation? Why then would the Holy Spirit lead Jesus directly into the wilderness where He was exposed to Satan's temptations?

This description of Jesus' baptism, and subsequent temptation in the wilderness, parallels another account in the scriptures where there is a reference to being "led into the wilderness." The number 40 is also mentioned: "And you shall remember all the way which the LORD your God *led* you these *forty* years in the *wilderness*, to humble you, and to prove you, that you might *know* what was in your heart, whether you would keep His commandments, or not. And He humbled you, and let you be hungry, and gave you manna to eat, a food which neither you nor your fathers knew, so that He might make you know that man does not live by bread alone, but he lives by every word that proceeds out of the mouth of the Lord."[10]

Does this mean that Jesus needed to be humbled and proven trustworthy to see whether or not He would keep His Father's commandments? Interestingly, the Hebrew verb *led* literally means "to carry or to bring,"[11] and the verb *to humble* can also be translated "to exercise or to train."[12] The verb *to prove* includes the meaning "to test or to appraise"[13] while the Hebrew verb *to keep* carries the idea of "to guard or to protect."[14] Thus, an alternate reading of this reference from Deuteronomy could be rendered: "And you shall be mindful of the ways which the Lord your God bore you these forty years in the wilderness to exercise you and to appraise you that *you* might know what was in your heart, whether or not you would guard His commands. So He put you through a training exercise during which He let you go hungry and fed you with manna, a new experience for you which your fathers were not familiar with, in order that you would know that your life is not sustained merely with natural food, but that you live by every word that is proceeding from the mouth of Jehovah [I AM]."

Earlier a reference was made to the fact that Jesus had to learn obedience: "Though He was a Son, yet He *learned obedience* through the suffering He endured."[15] This word *obedience* is the Greek word *hupakoe,* which literally means "to listen attentively so as to comply."[16] This scripture plainly states that through testing as a human Jesus had to learn to pay attention to the voice of His Father in order to comply with His Father's will. This explains what His baptism of repentance was all about. His appointment with the devil was designed to establish and confirm His *hearing of* and *reliance upon* the Holy Spirit—the voice of the Father within Him. This was His repentance—the confirmation of His mind-set." The ability to please God comes by hearing His voice in our innermost being.

Repentance therefore is not so much what we do, as much as it is something we accept—a gift we receive. It is our surrender to the Gift of God within.[17] Repentance is the developmental process whereby our mind-set is brought to maturity, enabling us to hear and comply with the voice of God and to see the inner world of spirit. If this is the case, is it any wonder that before we can enter the kingdom of heaven (the promised land of rest), we also will have to undergo a baptism of repentance? Jesus referred to the certainty of such a baptism when he said, "You shall indeed drink of My cup, and be baptized with the baptism that I am baptized with."[18]

Referring back to what John said in Matthew's account, we see a parallel description regarding those who would receive the baptism with which Jesus would baptize them. It seems clear that all who truly "follow" Christ will be tried and purged by fire: "He shall baptize you with the Holy Spirit and with fire. Whose winnowing fork is in His hand, and He will thoroughly purge His floor, and gather His wheat into the granary; but He will burn up the chaff with unquenchable fire."[19] This reference to a "winnowing fork in His hand" may well be an allegorical reference to the agents (human and demonic) by which we are tried in "the fiery trial of our faith,"[20] a faith which not only enables us to see the kingdom of heaven but empowers us to enter and abide there.

The evidence points to the fact that our entrance into the kingdom is possible only after the chaff of our fallen mind-set, our rational conception of self (our false identity), is completely burned away to give place to a brand-new supernatural perception of who we really are in Christ: "Whatsoever is born of God is a new creature!"[21] This is a direct reference to the inner awakening that allows us to see ourselves for who we truly are!

Jesus overcame the devil's temptation by learning to listen and comply with the *Rhema* (the speaking) of God within Him. Only then did He become fully fixed in His earthly identity as "the Son of Man." In other words, upon His repentance (His exchange of mind), He was capable of not only seeing the kingdom of heaven, but He was empowered to enter and walk in that kingdom with authority and grace as a man! Although "seeing" the kingdom is not the same as entering it, it is necessary to see the kingdom within in order to enter it.

Later on, subsequent to His baptism of repentance in the Spirit, Jesus discloses the modus operandi by which He lived and ministered. He revealed that He walked with an inner sight of the kingdom: "The Son can do nothing of Himself, except what He *sees* the Father doing: for whatever the Father does, this also the Son does likewise."[22] Another witness of the fact that Jesus walked in the sight of a heavenly kingdom is recorded in Mark's Gospel: "And when He had taken the five loaves and the two fishes, He *looked up* to heaven, and blessed, and broke the loaves, and gave them to His disciples to set before them; and the two fishes divided He among them all."[23] The verb *looked up* when literally translated means "to receive sight" or "to recover sight."[24] Jesus not only saw heaven, but He walked in heaven while on earth—a kingdom that He came to introduce to mankind.

Jesus walked in a real kingdom realm that He beheld with His inner sight. This explained the power of His earthly ministry as a man. The record indicates that this inner sight was "born" into Him by means of His baptism of repentance in the Spirit. His entrance into this kingdom was contingent upon the testing that this baptism brought about and His response to that trial by fire. In other words, it was His baptism of repentance and immersion in the Spirit that translated Jesus into the kingdom of heaven on earth.

Notes

1   Heb. 4:15

2   Matt. 3:15

3   Heb. 5:8

4   2 Cor. 7:10

5   Strong's (3340)

6   Luke 1:35, italics added

7   Mark 1:12,13, italics added

8   Strong's (1544)

9   Mark 1:39

10   Deut. 8:2,3 italics added

11   Strong's (03212)

12   Strong's (06031)

13   Strong's (03254)

14   Strong's (08104)

15   Heb. 5:8, italics added

16   Strong's (5218)

17   Rom. 2:4; 2 Tim. 2:25

18   Matt. 20:23

19   Matt. 3:11b,12

20   1 Pet. 4:12

21　2 Cor. 5:17
22　John 5:19, italics added
23　Matt. 14:19, italics added
24　Strong's (308)

Chapter 9

True Repentance

The question before us now is why is repentance necessary in order to enter the kingdom of heaven? Our ability to walk in the kingdom of heaven is contingent upon whether we have repented to the point of knowing who we are. True repentance inevitably transforms our identity because it affects how we perceive ourselves. It determines *who* we perceive ourselves to be. Before we are able to enter the kingdom of heaven, at some point in our growth and development, each of us must, with mature insight, answer the fundamental question: "Who am I?"

Within each of us, there is a faculty of our personality that images who we are. This inner imaging faculty is better known as our imagination. In most cases our imagination has been prostituted to our false identity and therefore must be sanctified—set apart for our true Self. When we look into a physical mirror, we naturally see ourselves reflected. The question here is when we behold the image in the mirror within our inner being, who does this inner mirror consistently reveal we are? This is to say, who do we perceive ourselves to be in our innermost being? Who do we see reflected? As long as our thinker is allowed to govern our lives, our imagination inevitably reflects the vain reasoning of our rational mind, portraying us as independent, separate selves. But when we have repented and our thinker has learned to submit to our Knower, our imagination reflects our true Self.

Scripture refers to this imaging faculty in the following terms: "Beholding the glory of the I AM reflected as in a mirror, we are thereby transformed into the exact same image from glory to increasing glory as by the Spirit."[1] It is the image portrayed in our imagination that reveals our identity. The reflection we behold in the mirror indicates who we image ourselves to be.

The inevitable question is who do we perceive ourselves to be? Are we aware of our true Self? Are we conscious of our real identity as I AM, or do we merely conceive of ourselves as autonomous human beings? We will either be unconsciously imagining the illusion of a separated, independent self, founded on the conceptions of our rational mind or, having surrendered our mind to the presence of I AM within, we will have awakened to our true sense of self, beholding the image of our true I AM within. In this conscious state of being, our inner sight will bear witness to the undeniable fact that we have been reconciled, i.e., made one with the One.[2] We will perceive ourselves in union with the I AM—our identity as Him![3] In so doing, we will have become one with our Head and thus identify ourselves as body members of Christ Himself, sharing one common life. Failing such an awakening, we will continue to dream a dream that imagines each person to be a broken-off, independent self, merely one of many such imaginary separate selves.

Once we have truly repented, we will "no longer see any person after the flesh."[4] We will know in our Knower that there is only one I AM—one Center from which all human life is lived! For truly there is only one self-sufficient Self in the whole universe! As we learn to live from this common Center consistently so as to derive our sense of self from the "I AM the I AM,"[5] we will not only have access to the kingdom of heaven, but we will walk in the power of that kingdom as fully privileged citizens of heaven!

Jesus, as a man, knew who He was. More than eighty times in the Gospels, He refers to Himself as "the Son of Man." It is significant to note that He was not born with this identity. His identity as the Son of Man was an identity Jesus had to learn. It was an identity He learned through the testing and temptation that He endured. Scripture documents that Jesus was born with the identity of "the Son of God," as recorded in Luke's Gospel account: "And the angel answered and said unto her, 'The Holy Spirit shall *come in* upon [literally *impregnate*[6]] you, and the power of the Highest shall overshadow you: therefore also that holy thing which will be born of you shall be called *the Son of God*.'"[7] Jesus' experience in the wilderness brought Him to repentance, confirming Him to walk beyond the scope of His rational mind, in a stereo consciousness with His Father and the human race.

As Jesus was about to return to His preincarnate state, He announced to His followers: "And you shall receive supernatural power after the Holy Spirit has *come in upon* [same word as in the previous scripture, *impregnated*[8]] you, and you will be witnesses of the I AM."[9] Just as surely as the power of the Holy Spirit raised up a physical birth of the Son of God in Mary's womb, just as surely does this same Spirit raise up a spiritual birth of this same I AM within the hearts of those who repent of their false identities and receive Him as their I AM. In the same manner that Mary surrendered to the word of the angel, even so must be the response of those who receive the indwelling I AM as their life: "Behold the servant of the Lord; be it unto me according to your spoken word [Greek, *Rhema*]."[10]

As a member of the human race, Jesus, like anyone else, had to learn what it meant to be a human being. Through the baptism of repentance, which He experienced, He learned His identity as the Son of Man. This was "the righteousness which He had to fulfill"[11] as a man. This is the obedience Jesus had to learn. We, on the other hand, are born into the false identity of a separate, independent son of man. It is our identity as a "son of God" (literally, a kin of God [12]) that we must learn by the testing and trials that we suffer.

Only our testing by fire will reveal our true identity as human sons and daughters of God. Only a baptism by fire in the Spirit will make the kingdom of heaven accessible to us, by consuming the dross of our false conceptions of self, revealing our true I AM within. As we go through the fire of our baptism of repentance, we begin to distinguish what is real and what is a shadow of the real. We begin to discern what spirit is and what soul is. It is only this division between soul and spirit that will enable us to walk in the stereo consciousness of abundant life. This state of *being*, in which the thinker is brought under the Knower, will alone enable us to walk in union with God.

This fully awakened conscious state arises within as the rational mind learns to become subservient to, and fully confident in, the true I AM who comprises the core of our being. Only when the independent thinking of the soul is broken, like a wild horse broken of its unruliness, is the soul liberated from its bondage to corruption and set free into the limitless reality of the kingdom of heaven. True repentance is the process by which this paradigm shift from thinking to knowing takes place. We have truly repented when we identify with knowing rather than thinking.

If Jesus' baptism necessitated His being led into the wilderness to be tried and tempted by the devil, we should not be surprised if, and when, our baptism of repentance in the Spirit becomes a baptism by fire, which straightway leads us through the valley of the shadow of death. In other words, our being born into the kingdom will require a scheduled encounter with the devil and his demons in the wilderness. Jesus said this very thing to Peter, "Satan has desired you to sift you as wheat, but I have prayed for you that your faith would not fail."[13] It is this experience of aloneness with the wild beasts of the spirit realm where we will be tried and tested in order to burn off all the dross and consume all the chaff of our fallen mind-set. We must give up everything we inherited from our natural lineage and die to all that predisposes us to a false identity.

Without being freed from those false perceptions of who we imagine ourselves to be, those "high things that have exalted themselves against the knowing of God,"[14] we cannot enter the kingdom of heaven in the present moment. If Jesus' baptism in water and the Spirit took forty days to have its full effect, it should not cause us to wonder if our trial takes a while longer, seeing that it took forty years to have its full effect on that generation of Israelites who came out of Egypt. Although it took only a matter of weeks to orchestrate the exodus of the children of Israel out of Egypt, it took forty years to get Egypt out of the Israelites. Only when their mind-set, their perception of reality, was radically changed were they prepared to enter the Land of Promise!

The following scriptures bear witness to the fact that it is our baptism by fire that confirms our entrance into the kingdom of heaven:

- Jesus said, "I have a baptism to be baptized with; and how constrained and perplexed I am until it is accomplished!"[15]
- Paul stated, "We *must* through much tribulation [anguish and pressure] enter into the kingdom of God."[16]
- Peter declared, "You have cause for great joy in this, though it may have been necessary for you to be distressed for a little while, being tested in all sorts of ways."[17]
- "Yes, and all who purpose to live in the knowledge of God in Christ Jesus [in the awareness of I AM] *will* suffer persecution."[18]
- "No one should be shaken by these afflictions: for you know yourself that *we are appointed* unto them."[19]
- "For *this is God's purpose* for you: because Christ also suffered for us, leaving us an example, that we should follow His steps."[20]
- "The afflictions of the righteous are many: but the LORD delivers them out of them all."[21]

- "I have given them Your word; and the world has hated them, because they are not of the world, even as I am not of the world."[22]
- "Those of us who live *are always set up and abandoned* unto death [to our false self] for Jesus' sake, *in order that* the life also of Jesus [the I AM within] might be made apparent in our mortal bodies."[23]
- "These things I have spoken unto you, that in Me [in I AM] you might have peace. In the world *you shall have tribulation*: but be of good cheer; I have overcome the world."[24]
- "You are of God, little children, and have overcome them: because greater is *I Am* who is in you, than the I am that is in the world."[25]
- "For the kingdom of God is not eating and drinking [not outward tangibility]; but righteousness, and peace, and joy in the Holy Spirit [inward reality]."[26]

Whenever we find ourselves abandoned in the fire of adversity, we need not lose heart. We can know in our Knower that we are being baptized into a new identity—an identity that is free from the tyrannical dictates of our rational mind. In my own case, I had never imagined how radically opposed my religious worldview was to the inner universe of spirit until adversity knocked on my door and revealed the absolute deficit in my capacity to love as God loves. It had never occurred to me that I had actually lived much of my life standing in opposition to the inner workings of I AM. I had been unconscious of His relentless attempts to bring me to that place of absolute and total dependency on His life within. I was too busy working *for* God—a distant, localized super deity who was nothing more than a figment of my imagination. Little did I know until then, all that was required of me was to abandon the life I had imagined was my own. In my unconsciousness, I had imagined all sorts of scenarios I thought would serve God's purpose, but in reality, all that was necessary was that I "sell all I had in exchange for the Treasure hidden within."[27]

At that point, the only thing I had, the only thing I could really call my own, was my imagined life—that life in which I had assumed an autonomous existence, in denial of the one true I AM.

It must be stated unequivocally here that there is no merit in suffering or persecution in and of themselves. Adversity can just as easily result in a person becoming hard and bitter as it can in one becoming kind and saintly. The benefit gained from hardships is due mainly to our response to what is happening in the moment. The power of transformation is not found in adversity per se, but in our identification with our true Self within. At best, difficult circumstances merely present us with opportunities to choose who we identify with–our created self or our divine Self—I am or I AM. In the same context, there is no gain realized by surrendering to a difficult situation. It is only in surrendering to the I AM who indwells the core of our being that we are empowered, in the midst of our trial, to overcome and rise above our circumstances. The power [the citizenship right] to abide in the kingdom of heaven flows directly from our identity, never from the circumstances we find ourselves in.

The evidence we have considered thus far could be summarized as follows. First, there is a kingdom to be entered today, in the here and now. Secondly, there is a baptism that we must undergo in order to enter this kingdom. The question we must ask ourselves at this juncture is, are we able to endure the required baptism? Jesus challenged His disciples with a similar question: "'You do not know what you ask. Are you able to drink of the cup that I shall drink of, and to be baptized with the baptism that I am baptized with?' They said unto Him, 'We are able.'" [28]

It will serve each of us well to consider the following questions: Have I ever really entered the kingdom of heaven? At this moment, am I living in the righteousness, peace, and joy of the Holy Spirit—the realities of which this kingdom consists? Am I among those living on planet Earth who have seen the kingdom of God come with power? Am I able to exercise the authority of this kingdom? Do I really know what I'm asking for when I unconsciously pray, "Thy kingdom come?"[29] Has it dawned on me that I too will have to be brought to repentance; kicking and screaming if need be, in order to enter the kingdom of heaven?

The kingdom of heaven is a real realm that exists in the here and now. It is our Father in heaven who alone can awaken us to this inner reality of life in union with I AM.

Notes

1   2 Cor. 3:18
2   Col. 1:21
3   1 John 4:17
4   2 Cor. 5:16
5   Exod. 3:14
6   Strong's (1904)
7   Luke 1:35, italics added
8   Strong's (1904)
9   Acts 1:8, italics added
10   Luke 1:38
11   Mark 3:15
12   Strong's (5207)
13   Luke 22:31,32
14   2 Cor. 10:15
15   Luke 12:50
16   Acts 14:22, italics added
17   1 Pet. 1:6
18   2 Tim. 3:12, italics added
19   1 Thess. 3:3, italics added
20   1 Pet. 2:21, italics added
21   Ps. 34:19
22   John 17:14
23   2 Cor. 4:11, italics added
24   John 16:33, italics added
25   1 John 4:4, italics added

26 Rom. 14:17
27 Matt. 13:44
28 Mark 10:38,39
29 Luke 11:2

Chapter 10

One Door into the Kingdom

I f God is a universal reality, could there be, according to the very nature of all things, more than one way to come to God? Would not the existence of a universal being necessitate a universal entrance into His presence? In acknowledging that God is a universal being, are we not in effect saying there is but one doorway into heaven?

To illustrate this point consider briefly the following example. Sunlight is a universal phenomenon. It is the same light that shines on the paved streets of New York city that shines in the rainforests of Southeast Asia. Sunlight is accessible in every corner of the globe. No matter where any creature lives on planet Earth, its "approach" to the light of the sun is one and the same—he, she or it must simply open their eyes in order to "enter into" this light. There is no other way for any creature to "come" to the light of the sun in order to comprehend the magnificent colors of the visible spectrum. There is only one door into the presence of the light—one gateway—the eye gate. Nature dictates that there is but one door.

The same principle of nature holds true with regard to "the Light of the world." By the very nature of our existence as human beings, in whom this inherent Light dwells, there is but one way to approach His Universal Presence. We must have our inner eyes opened to behold His imminent presence. There is no other doorway by which the Light can be known. To imagine that there is more than one such door into the presence of this Light is in essence to deny the existence of God Himself, who is, by definition, *the* Universal. Our thinking therefore must be reconciled to the fact that there is but one doorway into God's universal presence. It is equally certain that there could be only one universal entrance into the kingdom of heaven within.

The fact that Jesus Christ claimed to be this one universal entrance into heaven is undeniable. For He plainly declared, "I AM *the* entrance: through Me if any man enter in he shall be saved and shall enter in and come forth and discover the provision he has been searching for."[1] Although it seems clear enough from this statement that Jesus Christ is claiming in a very literal sense to *be* the one universal entrance into this kingdom of all sufficiency, in what sense can a person be the door into God's universal kingdom? What could Christ possibly mean by claiming to be the door into ultimate salvation and provision—the door into heaven? Many, including some Christians, find it extremely difficult to accept Jesus Christ's claim to be that one and only doorway into heaven, possibly because they consider Him purely from an outward, natural perspective. Most have never recognized who Jesus Christ really *is* because they have never understood His claim to be *the* I AM.

It is only natural for the rational mind, especially when conditioned by religion, to have great difficulty reconciling *personal* with *universal*. When we think of a person, we normally envision a localized being, an individual bound by time and space. Inversely, we conceptualize the universal in terms of that which is generic and nonpersonal. Consequently, to equate the person of Jesus Christ with the universal entrance into heaven is inconceivable for many. Yet it is this very inability to get beyond the confines of our traditional thought patterns that keeps us from seeing our true identity—seeing who we really are as a corporate being. The fact that we are stuck in our mind is precisely what necessitates our baptism by fire. The truth is our true identity cannot be defined in terms of rational concepts and intellectual constructs. Although we can illustrate our identity with intellectual conceptions, as we have said repeatedly, who we really are as a corporate being is beyond our rational thoughts. Our true identity, our real being, can only be understood in terms of knowing—in spirit.

To illustrate further what we are referring to in regard to a universal entrance, consider the following example. The Internet is a universal reality that is accessible globally. However, the Internet can only be accessed by one gateway—that prescribed protocol upon which the Internet is built. For instance, although I am sitting in a room that is fully accessible to the Internet (via the signal broadcast by my wireless router), I cannot get online and surf the net with either my VCR or my TV simply because they do not have the universal gateway built into them. However, with my computer or my Wi-Fi phone, I can log on to the Internet at any time because they are both configured with the universal gateway known as IPS (Internet Protocol System). This gateway is designed in accordance with the universal configuration of the Internet. In like manner, every human heart is "hardwired" with kingdom-access protocol. The gateway into the universal kingdom of heaven is the I AM at the core of our being. Christ Himself, the Light of the world, is the only possible way in, for He alone, as the universal I AM, dwells at the center of all human consciousness.

In order to facilitate this fundamental shift in our understanding, let's suggest something out of the ordinary. Let's consider the person of Jesus Christ in terms of the present moment. If this suggestion seems absurd to you, consider it in light of the following possibilities. Has it ever occurred to you that the present moment may be a crossroad where eternity intersects with time? Is it not feasible that this intersection, which we commonly refer to as the ever-present Now, might be a universal doorway into eternity? Combine this thought with the following queries: Have you ever considered that I AM is one and the same as the eternal present? By claiming to be the I AM, is it not possible that Jesus Christ is claiming to be the personification of the present moment—the universal entrance into eternity? If we can accept Jesus Christ's claim to be *the* I AM, surely it is not too much of a stretch to equate His "I AM-ness" with the present moment, or a universal doorway.

The plausibility of equating Jesus Christ with the present moment is confirmed by how Jesus presented Himself to the religious leaders who opposed Him relentlessly. He declared to them openly that once He retreated from their visible sight, they would not be able to follow Him nor find Him, unless they understood what He was saying to them in that moment. In plain language, He referred to Himself in this universal sense when He said, "When I withdraw out of sight you will seek Me and you will die in your sin; for where I withdraw to you won't be able to come. Then the Jews said, 'Will he kill Himself?' because He said, 'Where I withdraw to you won't be able to come.' Then Jesus said to them, 'You are from beneath I am from above. You are of this realm I am not of this realm.' This is why I said; 'You will die in your sins,' for if you do not believe that I AM, you will die in your sin."[2]

Is not Jesus saying here that salvation (freedom from SIN) is found in recognizing Him as I AM? Is not the I AM one and the same as the present? In other words, is He not indicating that the entrance into heaven is Himself, the I AM, the ever-present Now, a door which will not be accessible any other opportunity than now? The point here is if Jesus Christ truly is the I AM, in a universal sense, then it is only reasonable to conclude that He Himself is the one and only entrance into eternity.

In fact, once the fire of our baptism has consumed the chaff of our fallen perceptions, i.e., our false sense of identity, we actually discover that our true I AM has been waiting for us to come to Him within. Did Jesus not clearly state that whoever believed in (literally *into*) Him would find rivers of living water flowing from within their own being?[3] How could such a fountain spring up from within unless its source was inherently there?[4] Is He not here revealing that He, as the I AM, dwells at the core of all human consciousness?

He, as the ever-present Now, is the one door that exists between the temporal reality of this material world and the eternal kingdom of heaven. The scripture is clear that there is no salvation available to the human race outside of the Present Moment: "Behold, *now* is the accepted time; behold, *now* is the opportunity for salvation."[5] This Now is none other than the I AM: "And in no other is there salvation, for there is no other name [person] under heaven, given among [literally within] men, in whom we must have salvation."[6] In other words, the Now and Christ are not two different realities, but one and the same. Christ is the Now! He is the I AM—the Present Moment!

This entrance into the kingdom of heaven is not an exclusive door open only to a select few who adhere to the creeds of a particular organized religion. Because of what Jesus Christ the Man accomplished in his conception, birth, life, death, resurrection, and ascension, this entrance stands open at the core of every human heart. The door is the I AM of every man's existence—the core Self that our false identity has blinded us to and robbed us of. "He is the Light of the world—the Light [the core consciousness] who lights *every* man who comes into the world. Although He had always been in the world [i.e., the inhabitants—each and every person] the world did not know [perceive or comprehend] Him."[7]

Our baptism by fire, therefore, is not an arbitrary initiation required of us by a capricious deity who impulsively decides who will get into heaven and who will not. By the very nature of all things, our trial by fire is the one inherent requirement necessary to enable us to recognize this inner door into the kingdom. This baptism alone can empower us to enter the reality at the center of our being. Without repentance—without this exchange of mind—there is no possibility of recognizing the Present Moment for who He really is. Except for this radical paradigm shift in our inner awareness, there is no prospect of being saved from the illusion of our false sense of self—that illusionary identity that is the mother of all evil, chaos, and death.

This is precisely why Jesus said, "How hard is it for those who trust in their own wealth to enter into the kingdom of God"[8] and conversely, "Blessed are the poor in spirit: for theirs is the kingdom of heaven."[9] As long as we are rich in our own estimation of ourselves, we cannot see or enter the kingdom of heaven on earth. The more resources we have at our disposal to support our false sense of self, the less likely we are to give up all that is needful to enter the real world within.

It is impossible to live in two opposing paradigms. In other words, no one can have two core identities. Jesus put it this way, "No man can serve two masters."[10] By the very nature of the universal reality of the kingdom of God, there is no feasible way for one who believes in more than one "I am" to live in the reality of One. There is only one I AM. In other words, there is only one self-sufficient person in the whole universe. By the very nature of the name I AM, there could not be more than one! This is evident in how Jehovah introduced Himself to the prophet Moses: "I AM *the* I AM."[11] He revealed Himself in much the same way to the prophet Isaiah: "I AM *the* I AM, and there is *no one else*, besides Me there is no God; I AM your strength though you do not know Me, that men may know, from the rising of the sun and from the west, that there is *no one besides Me*; I AM *the* I AM, and *there is no one else*. I form light and create darkness, I make peace and create calamity, I AM *the* I AM, who does all these things."[12]

Although many of the I AM claims which Jesus Christ made regarding Himself are hidden in English translations of the scriptures, for any genuine student of history, it would be impossible to overlook the number and the magnitude of these claims. In order to make Jesus' declarations make sense to the thinker, most translators have added the word "he" following "I AM" so that it reads, "I am *he*." However, in the original Greek text the intended meaning is clear. To ignore such blatant megalomania on His part and simply classify Jesus Christ as an enlightened teacher is either misguided ignorance of what He claimed to be, or it is to suggest that all men are equally almighty gods in their own right, which is even more absurd. Either Christ is that one universal I AM in human form, which He claimed to be, or He is a madman with psychotic delusions, whose memory deserves to be obliterated from human history.

When Jesus Christ says, "I am *the* way, *the* truth and *the* life, no man comes to the Father but by Me,"[13] is He not in plain language claiming to be the one universal way to God? Is He not also blatantly declaring Himself to be the one universal life of all living things, as well as the embodiment of absolute truth? How can anyone classify such claims as enlightenment unless these declarations actually describe the nature of the one who made them? On the other hand, if these claims are true, then there are some radical adjustments needed in our inmost sense of self.

For truly, if Jesus Christ is the I AM, as He claims, then it would follow that to be conscious of Him as our true center is to walk in "the way." Could this be what Jesus meant when He said, "If you *abide in Me* you will bear much fruit"[14]? This fruit is produced in the same way fruit is produced on the branches of a tree, by the flow of the Spirit of Christ through us empowering us to live in conscious union with Him. Is this not what Jesus meant when He said, "The Spirit of truth will guide you into all reality, revealing Me within as your life."[15]?

If Jesus Christ is I AM, then to abide in Him is the same as to live consciously in the Now. It also follows that if I AM is the universal door then to live in the Now is evidently the one and only way into the kingdom of God. In fact being present in the moment is not only the entrance into the kingdom, but it is also to walk in the way of the kingdom. For it is a self-evident fact that all of life is lived only in the present moment. The only real life that exists is now—in this moment! There is no other life except in the Now! Yesterday is only a memory of now; tomorrow is an imagination, which isn't real until it's now. I AM is all there is. He is the only real time we have. To live anywhere but the Now is to live in an illusion. It is to live a lie.

The amazing thing to consider is that the kingdom of heaven is open to everyone in this present moment. This door called I AM is accessible to every person. It is possible right now for anyone of us who is ready to step into our true Self, our real identity, to be free from the dominating thoughts of our minds that keep us locked into a false perception. There exists at the core of our being a secret place of blessed heavenly rest that many have failed to enter and that most have unconsciously resisted entering. This place of repose is available to whoever desires to cease from themselves:

> Seeing therefore that some still need to enter this rest and because those to whom this rest was first announced refused to enter because of disbelief [willful unconsciousness], He appoints another opportunity saying; *Today*, even after such a long time it is still: *Today*, if you will listen to the sound of His voice, do not resist in your heart. Truly there remains this Sabbath rest to the people of God. Whoever has entered into His rest has *ceased* from his own activity, even as God did from His. So let us hasten to move into this rest, lest anyone of us fall into the same pattern of disbelief [willful unconsciousness].[16]

Note carefully that the entrance into this heavenly rest of the soul has always been today. It is always Now! Ever since the beginning of creation, the entrance into this secret place of the soul has always been the present moment. Clearly, there is no other entrance into this promised heavenly rest than through the I AM! The kingdom of heaven in our midst has but one door, it is the Now. This Sabbath rest of the soul is not merely to be observed on the seventh day or one day in seven, but is accessible in the present—24/7.

The *ceasing* referred to here does not mean merely to cease from outward activity but from our own inward activity. It is to cease from ourselves. It means to cease from our own thoughts that imprison us in ignorance, blindness, and death. This is not to suggest that we cease thinking, which would be a ludicrous impossibility. It simply means we cease living out of our own mind, out of our own intellect. We give up being controlled by our thinker by learning to be governed by our Knower. We become identified with our real Self rather than merely with whom we think we are. This means all our judgments and determinations now arise out of our true identity, the I AM, rather than originating from our broken-off, independent sense of self—our own illusionary I am. Rather than living from the *independence* of our own thinking, we live *in dependence* upon our inner knowing. We walk in the spirit, not according to the dictates of the intellectual mind (which scripture calls the flesh).[17] In this rest, our intellect is governed by our true Self. "Christ-in-us, *as us,* the hope of glory"[18] is the one door into the kingdom! This door is here, in the present moment. The door is Now. There is only one Now.

Notes

1   John 10:9, italics added

2   John 8:21-24

3   John 7:38

4   John 4:14

5   2 Cor. 6:2, italics added

6   Acts 4:12

7   John 1:2,9,10, italics added

8   Mark 10:24

9   Mark 5:3

10   Matt. 6:24

11   Exod. 3:14, italics added

12   Isa. 45:5-7, italics added

13   John 14:6

14   John 15:5, italics added

15   John 16:13,14, paraphrased

16   Heb. 4:6-11, italics added

17   Rom. 8:5-8

18   Col. 1:27, italics added

Chapter 11

The Price of the Kingdom

In view of the foregoing evidence, we are encouraged to endure the fire of our baptism in order to partake of the glory of the kingdom within:

> Beloved, do not think it strange concerning the fiery trial which is designed to prove you, as though some strange thing is happening to you. But rejoice in the fact that you are partakers of Christ's sufferings [His entrance into the heavenly kingdom]; so that when His glory is revealed in you, you may be glad and jump for joy. If you are defamed as Christ, you are blessed; for *the Spirit of glory and of God refreshes you*. On their part I AM is vilified, but on your part He [in you] shows up gloriously.[1]

As we've seen, scripture makes it clear that everyone who lives in union with the I AM will be tested in the fire. It also declares that everyone's work will go through the fire in order to reveal the delusion and/or reality of every man's state of being:

Every man's work shall be made apparent: for the day shall declare it, because it shall be revealed by fire; and the fire shall try every man's work to see what sort it is. If any man's work comes through the test, he will have a reward. If the fire puts an end to any man's work, it will be his loss: yet he himself will be saved, though as by fire.[2]

It is not only the substance of our works that will be revealed in the final judgment at the end of the age, but our thoughts also will be revealed by the fire in the day of our baptism. It is written that "judgment must begin at the house of the Lord."[3] We are that house. We, as humans, were created as the living sanctuary of the indwelling Deity.[4] Our baptism of repentance is tailored to expose the fallacy of our imagined identity and thereby open the one and only entrance into the eternal kingdom to all who are ready to enter. This kingdom reality, which abides in the midst of our being, is accessible only in the Present Moment—only through Christ, our I AM. We have the choice to either react against the fire of our baptism or to respond to the fire in the moment.

Scripture states clearly that man was designed to manifest the magnificent splendor of the indwelling Deity: "Are you unconscious that your body exists as the shrine of the Holy Spirit within you? What you have is given by God, hence you are not your own. In fact, you are bought with a price: therefore allow the splendor of God to be apparent in your body, and in your spirit, which are God's."[5] Due to this inherent divine nature, the true power of the human soul can only ever be realized in its surrender to a power that is greater than itself. This statement is of such profound significance that it will help to rephrase it. The entire sphere of our human choice is either to surrender to I AM in the fire or resist the fire and miss the I AM. We resist because our mind sees the fire as a threat to our false identity. Yet even though self-determination seems like the right way it is always diametrically opposed to the soul's best interests. As imperceptible as our choices may seem, our freedom from SIN (our salvation from our false self) is only ever found in the Present Moment—by surrendering to the I AM.

The kingdom is open to all who will walk through the fire into their true I AM! The fiery furnace into which Shadrach, Meshach, and Abednego of old were thrown,[6] is a picture of our baptism in the fire. The fire they walked through merely consumed the bonds that restricted them, setting them free to walk with the Son of God, unharmed in the midst of the fire. Our baptism in the fire will do the same for us, consuming the confining structures in our mind that stand in resistance to the being of God at our core. As these three men surrendered their lives to God in the fire and walked with God in the midst of the furnace, accepting our baptism will release us to walk in the presence of I AM whose love nature is a consuming fire.[7]

Several questions each of us would do well to consider personally:

- Have I entered through the door of the I AM?
- Am I walking in the way of the kingdom of heaven?
- Am I dwelling in the here and now?
- Am I abiding in the present moment?

If not, there remains a place of rest and peace for anyone who will take it. This door is open to whoever chooses to enter it. However, due to the fundamental nature of our humanity, whatever we surrender our souls to will ultimately conquer our souls.[8] Whatever we take, in the end, will take us. In other words, there will be a price to pay.

You may be wondering why this inner door remains such a great mystery to most. If this door is so universally accessible why do so few ever seem to find their way into the kingdom of heaven. The reason so few even search for this door is because of the price that is required to enter it. Jesus explained it in the following terms: "Crowded with obstacles is the door and restricted with trouble is the way that leads to life, and only a small number bother to make the discovery of it."[9] The door into the kingdom is well guarded with trouble, and the way of the kingdom is inundated with affliction. Only those who chose to surrender to their baptism of fire are able to find the door and enter therein. The trouble and affliction we encounter upon our entrance to this inner kingdom are primarily due to the perceptions (and the experience) of the false self that must be brought to death in order that we may enter with our true identity. For it is certain that "the natural man cannot inherit the kingdom of God."[10] We simply can't get in with a counterfeit ID.

Although everyone is free to enter, the kingdom of heaven comes at a considerable cost. Our entrance will cost us everything—everything we call our "own." This is not merely a reference to outward things, the stuff of this world. *Everything* in this case goes far beyond material possessions. It refers to all that bolsters our false image of self—every thought and attitude that sustains our thinker as the arbitrator of our life. It includes every imagination that maintains our illusionary identity. In this case, *everything* includes every mind structure and intellectual construct that stands in support of who we *think* we are.

The apostle Paul described the experience of his baptism in the fire in these terms:

> Without doubt I consider *everything* that is gain to me [everything that sustains my false sense of being] as a write-off in exchange for the supreme knowing of Christ, for whom I have suffered the loss of everything, that I may gain Christ [as my identity] and be found *in* Him [one with Him] not having my *own* righteousness which is based on my performance, but that which is through the faith of Christ [in me], the righteousness of God Himself through faith. That I may know Him [the I AM], and the power of His resurrection, and the fellowship of His sufferings [His trials and death], being assimilated into His death; if by any means I might attain unto the resurrection of the dead [in the here and now]. Not as though I had already attained, nor were already perfect:

but I press forward in order to lay hold of that [identity]
for which Jesus Christ laid hold of me.[11]

One question that presents itself here is if the rational mind
cannot inherit the kingdom, how will we know whether we have
entered the kingdom of heaven? We will know by the number of
deaths we have died to our false self life. We will know that we
have entered reality when the fire has taken from us all that is
not real. In other words, we will know that we have paid the full
price, only by what we have given up in exchange for it. The true
value of anything is always realized in terms of what is given in
exchange for it. When we have escaped the tyranny of our natural
mind and entered into the I AM of our true being, we will know
that we have paid the ultimate price. At that point, we will not
only have partaken of the crucifixion of Christ, but we will have
entered into the power of His resurrection. In the fire, we will have
died and been reborn from above. We will have been translated
from the power of darkness into the kingdom of light. Only then
will we live in heaven on earth!

Jesus reveals the price of the kingdom in this parable: "Again,
the kingdom of heaven is like a treasure hidden in a field; which
when a man has found, he hides, and with great joy goes and sells
all that he has, and buys that field. Again, the kingdom of heaven is
like a merchant man, seeking rare pearls: Who, when he had found
one pearl of great price, went and sold *all that he had*, and bought
it."[12] The field in which we find this hidden treasure is nowhere
distant to any one of us—it is our human soul. For this is where
the kingdom is found, at the center of our being! The one way to
enter this kingdom, to purchase this pearl of great price, is to give
up *all* that we have. The only thing we can really call our own is
our mistaken identity. We must relinquish our whole sense of self.
For even if we give all our material possessions to the poor, we have
not really given up anything significant unless we have given up
who we think we are. The only currency with which we can "buy

the field" is our false sense of self. Our only way to "purchase the pearl" is to part with the illusion that our individuality is founded on an independent will—an "own" right to self-determination.

Until we lose our own life, renounce our fake ID, we cannot follow I AM. We cannot be His disciples unless we disown that identity that stands in denial of His universal I AM-ness—that sense of self that was built and is maintained by the thought structures of our fallen mind. Jesus told His disciples, "If any man desires to accompany Me, let him deny [disown or abstain from] his own self, and take up his cross daily, and follow Me."[13] We cannot put the new wine of life in Christ into the old wine skins of our rational perception of ourselves.[14] For this false life is nothing more than a house of cards built on the sand, a house that the fire will reveal as chaff and vanity.

Scripture makes this exit from "own self" into HIMSELF abundantly clear when it speaks of the Sabbath rest of the soul:

> If during the Sabbath rest you keep from going your *own* way, not doing your *own* pleasure on My holy day; and call for the Sabbath rest to be a delight, holy to the Lord, a celebration to be honored; and if you give respect to Him by not doing your *own* ways, or going after your *own* pleasure, or saying your *own* words; then I AM will be your delight and I will make you ride the high places of the earth and feed you with the heritage of Jacob your father; for the mouth of I AM has spoken it.[15]

Note how many times we are called to relinquish *own*. In literal terms, we are called to disown all of independent self—to deny everything that supports own self. As noted earlier this observance of the Sabbath is not a call to abstain from *own* one day in seven but includes every moment of every day.

It is important to note that this reference to "losing our own life and denying ourselves" does not mean that we commit mental, emotional or physical suicide—that we deny the existence of our humanity, our soul life. We are offspring of Deity. As finite created souls, we have inherited our Father's divinity. We are human souls created in His divine image—birthed to express His divine nature. It would be utter foolishness to imagine that we could shed our humanity in order to become almighty Deity. Only senseless pride would suggest we could claim divinity for ourselves by denying that we are finite human creatures.

What we must deny is the soul's seizure of headship over spirit—the soul's assumption to independent godhood. Our humanity was never designed to rule over our divinity but to be subservient to it, in much the same way light reigns over darkness in the realm of materiality. When darkness reigns it produces death and chaos. When Light reigns it does not annihilate darkness; it merely subjugates it and thereby transforms it, revealing its true potential. An example of this is the sun's rays shining on the petals of a red rose. If the darkness in the rose could rule over the sunlight, not only would it never allow the true beauty of color hidden in the light to be revealed, but it would also rob the rose of its one and only source of life. For the splendor of color and the manifold wonder of life is not in the rose but in the sunlight alone. Like the rose, we are birthed as manifestors of the Light who lights every man.

It was the introduction of the virus called SIN (Satan's Incarnate Nature) that inverted the original order of man's inner constitution. It is this false sense of I am-ness (idolatry) that is the root of all evil and chaos in the universe. In the beginning, when man's divinity ruled over his humanity, he walked with God.[16] In other words, he walked in conscious union with Deity. He was never designed to walk in autonomy, consciously separated from his indwelling divinity. As evidenced in the life of Jesus Christ who described Himself as "the Father manifested in the flesh," man was created to be an individual expression of the one universal I AM in human form. This is man's true inheritance. Lost paradise cannot be regained without giving up his false ID. This is the price of the kingdom, a price which, amazingly enough, has been paid in full! Our choice is simply to surrender to what is or to maintain the illusion by our self-determination.

Notes

1   1 Peter 4:13,14, italics added
2   1 Cor. 3:13,14
3   1 Peter 4:17
4   1 Cor. 3:16; 1 Pet. 2:5
5   1 Cor. 6:19,20
6   Dan. 3:12-30
7   1 John 4:16; Heb. 12:29
8   Rom. 6:16
9   Matt. 7:13,14
10   1 Cor. 15:50
11   Phil. 3:7-12, italics added
12   Matt. 13:44-46, italics added
13   Luke 9:2,3
14   Luke 5:38
15   Isa. 58:13,14, italics added
16   Gen. 3:8

Chapter 12

Presence

There are some realities in the realm of spirit that are virtually impossible to describe with human language. The best that vocabulary can do in explaining these infinite realities is point to that which is beyond words. If we are mindful of this fact, it can be helpful at times to "walk around" these invisible truths, pointing to them with as many words as possible. In such cases, the words are used merely to entice the reader to look past the terminology into the realm of spirit where these actualities exist. If the thinker is allowed to arbitrate in such cases, the words used to describe infinite reality will merely contribute to more intellectual structures that will stand in the way of seeing the spiritual landscape. Therefore, if we desire to develop our inner senses to experience reality, it is imperative that the thinker give way to the Knower.

A case in point is the reality of Presence. In order to reflect on the following description of this eternal truth, it is essential to step beyond the boundaries of our rational learning. Do not let your mind get hung up on the terms used but rather open the eyes of your heart to observe the actual reality of Presence in the inner realm of spirit.

Look at the words merely as signposts, pointing to a destination that is infinitely beyond the veil of rational thought. Here then are some pointers to this invisible reality called Presence.

Presence is the infinite space in which the unfolding sequence of life emerges. It is that universal atmosphere in which the flowering of human awareness blossoms into its full glory. However, Presence is not only the environment in which everything has existence; it is the structure that permeates everything that has form. It is not merely a universal force or an inert energy but an infinitely personal being. Presence is the stillness inhabiting the core of our existence, giving us the light of life. It is that inmost state of being residing at the root of our awareness. Presence is the root consciousness, the Ultimate Observer, standing observant behind the constant surge of all our thoughts.

To be present therefore is to be fully conscious in the moment—to be wholly aware of our individuality within the Universal Self. It is to be conscious of the events of our individual life as they become known within that concourse we call here and now—the Present Moment. Being present is the habitual practice of abiding in conscious union with the ever-present I AM. To practice Presence, therefore, is to consciously and consistently present our created self to the universal reality of I AM within—allowing our true Self to live His[A] infinite being through our

---

[A]   We refer to the infinite being of God with the masculine possessive pronoun "His", not to succumb to the patriarchal tradition of designating male gender at the exclusion of female, but mainly for lack of a better alternative. Rather than using the generic pronoun "it", which tends to present God as merely an impersonal energy field, we use the personal pronoun "He" to specify the reality of God's intelligent conscious personality. However, because of the historical connotations and cultural baggage associated with it, even the term "God" has lost much of its potency to unveil the invisible reality of infinite Being. More often than not, the term "God" conjures up the perception of a time/space bound being, rather than the universal personality of infinite Being.

Although Christ appeared in the form of a man, He readily attributed female characteristics to His personality. Much to the chagrin of His religious critics, He referred to His relationship with the infinite being of God in the context of Father/Son. By using the term Father His intention was not to promote male gender as more god-like than female, but to create an association in the minds of His followers that His inner conscious connection with the infinite being of God

individuality. Presence is that state of being where our soul is surrendered to spirit—our thinker subject to our Knower.

In view of our inescapable baptism by fire, it is to our great gain to abide in Presence by learning to accept the here and now as it is—for *who* He is! Rather than rejecting what is happening to us in the moment by complaining or wishing we were somewhere else or under different circumstances, our baptism enables us to see the benefit in saying yes to the Now. For in refusing to reconcile with the Now, we unconsciously resist "Him who effectually *works all things* according to the counsel of His own determination."[1]

The rational mind naturally judges circumstances and events in terms of how they concern our false identity. If what is happening in the moment in any way diminishes or threatens our counterfeit sense of self, the thinker unconsciously labels it as bad or evil and rejects it. On the other hand, if the events of the Present Moment support our false sense of self, the thinker labels them good, thereby reinforcing our mistaken identity.

In our real Self we recognize the Present Moment as the sole continuum in which human being can be experienced—the only opportunity to participate in real Life. Rather than accept the mind's verdict that the present moment is good or bad, we can choose to identify with our true I AM. As we learn to relinquish the intellectual perceptions of our thinker unto the inner knowing that is emerging within, we experience Life Himself in the moment. By simply surrendering the judgment calls of our thinker to the discernment of our I AM within, we choose Life. For He alone is life![2]

Even if our mind persists in labeling what is happening in the moment as bad or evil, in our true Self, we accept it, receiving it as

---

had all the characteristics we would naturally attribute to a relationship with a perfect loving human father.

Throughout scripture the infinite being of Deity is portrayed, not only with paternal attributes, but often with maternal characteristics and instincts as well. However, this does not mean God is both male and female, for God is neither masculine or feminine. Although the infinite nature of God can be clearly understood through either or both genders, the being of God is as far beyond gender as infinite is beyond finite.

"God working all things together for good."[3] For we know that our baptism by fire is transmuting "our light affliction in the moment into a far more exceeding and eternal weight of glory."[4] This glory is not limited to the afterlife but also includes our participation in the glorious kingdom of God on earth, in the here and now.

Hence, we need no longer stay addicted to the illusive security of the mind's compulsive judgment calls. For our baptism of repentance presents us with the opportunity to step over into the consciousness of I AM where we literally "put on the mind of Christ"[5]—an awareness that empowers us to discern who we really are. Instead of relentlessly striving to become what we merely hoped to be in the future, we step over into the restful presence of being—being one with I AM, *now!* We step into knowing, no longer dominated by rational thought! We step into abundance and fullness here in this moment.

The unfortunate truth is, however, that not one of us gives up our mind-bound identity without a fight. For not only have we been born into our thinker, we have cherished the thoughts of our mind all our lives in the vain hope of becoming the person our mind can never allow us to be. It should be no surprise to us, therefore, that we may need some disciplines (training exercises) imposed on us to bring us to that place of repentance where we forsake our false identity. As the evidence implies, it is absolutely imperative that we go through the fire of trial and testing in order to be brought to the entrance—to that universal door into the real world. Nothing short of baptism in the fire will convince us to identify with the I AM—to accept the Present Moment for who He is.

We are disciplined in the fire to learn to "allow" the Present Moment to be as it is, no longer prejudiced by the opinion of the thinker. We learn to never allow our mind to have the final say in determining our response to what is happening to us in the moment. In other words, we learn not to mind the circumstances that envelop us. As we remain in this state of presence, our true I AM emerges from within, permeating our whole sense of being. His Presence in us, as our true Self, overcomes the challenges that confront us in the moment.

We move over into Presence simply by learning to reconcile with the Now as it is. The apostle Paul explains his relationship with the Now in the following terms:

> With great pleasure now will I boast about whatever exposes my own feebleness in the present moment, in order that the power of I AM may abide with me. So I take pleasure in being feeble, in unkind words, in needs, in cruel attacks, in troubles, on account of Christ: for when *I am* feeble, then *I AM* strong.[6]

Note Paul's reference to two "I am's." Here we see portrayed the proper relationship between soul and spirit—the thinker subject to Knower. This relationship between the two "I am's" is clearly evidenced in Paul's confession of faith in Christ where he said, "*I am* crucified in union with Christ [I AM], nevertheless *I* live, yet not *I*, but Christ [I AM] lives in *me* and the life *I* now live in the body *I* live by the faith of Christ [I AM] who loves me and gives *His life* in exchange for *my life*."[7]

By the very nature of all things then, the only logical thing we can do is "to present our own self [our thinker] as a living sacrifice, wholly acceptable to I AM [our Knower], which is our only logical worship,"[8] We make this living sacrifice by learning to say thank you for everything in the moment: "In everything giving thanks, for this *is* the pleasure of God *in* Christ Jesus concerning you!"[9] This "sacrifice of praise" is like shock treatment to the thinker. It brings the thinker under the Knower: "By Him [in Him, as Him], let us offer the *sacrifice of praise* to God every moment, that is, the fruit of our lips giving thanks to His name [literally, assenting to His person]."[10]

By receiving the moment with thankfulness in whatever form it presents itself to us, in whatever form He presents Himself to us, we remain Present. As we abide in Presence, saying yes to I AM in whatever circumstances we find ourselves, Life Himself rises up in us as our real Self. In this conscious union, abundant Life flows out through us, establishing us in our true identity. This new incarnate man, Christ-in-us, *as us*,[11] has the power to live victoriously above all circumstances: "You have overcome the false I am [Antichrist] because greater is *I AM* who is in you than *I am* who is in the world."[12] The only truly effective way to resist the world, the flesh, and the devil is to submit to I AM: "Submit your self to God and [thereby] resist the devil and he will vanish from you."[13] There is no lasting benefit in outwardly refusing to accept what we are identified with inwardly. We must inwardly disassociate our sense of self from the false I am by inwardly identifying with I AM. Herein lies our only power to overcome in our circumstances.

When we agree with our mind's desire to pass a verdict on the Present Moment, we fragment the continuity of inner space into isolated events. This fragmentation of the Now leaves us living in a broken-off mind-set that is separated from the ceaseless flow of Life Himself within. The thinker invariably perceives time as segmented—separated into past, present, and future. It is unconscious that time exists only in the present. It cannot know that there is no time except the Now. When we agree with our thinker in its labeling of the Present Moment as bad or evil, we reject the Now as it is. In other words, we literally say no to I AM as our Center—we deny the universal I AM and thus live in resistance to Presence.

Whether we profess to believe in Christ or not is of little consequence. Our refusal to abide in the I AM is, in all truth, a denial of Christ as Lord! Whenever we identify with our thinker, we are living in opposition to our true Self. Scripture refers to those who oppose their true selves: "In meekness instruct those who *oppose themselves*, if perhaps God will grant them repentance to the acknowledging of the Truth, that they may escape from the snare of the evil one [Satan's Incarnate Nature, the false self], ensnared by him to do his will."[14]

It is in this context that Jesus commanded His followers to "resist not evil, but whoever strikes you on your right cheek, turn to him the other also."[15] If we reject the Now, we live separated from our one and only real Life. In our separated thinking, we either become trapped in the past, regretting what might have been or we get lost in the future, wishing and hoping things to be other than they are in the present. We thus isolate ourselves from Life, we deny the Truth, and we reject the Way. Whenever we fail to abide in our Knower, we become unconscious—unconscious of I AM, unconscious of who we really are. We fall asleep to our true identity and re-enter the mind dream of the imagined. Living in our thinker confirms us in our false identity—that vain imagination in which we are convinced that we are separate selves in search of fulfillment. This false ID projects an identity that can only ever be realized at some point in the future.

On the other hand, when we allow the Fire to accomplish its objective through our baptism, we learn to appreciate the moment as is (as I AM). We begin to see that the Fire is not separate from the Now but one with the Moment. We recognize that the very nature of the I AM is Fire—a consuming Presence that metamorphoses our identity from I am to I AM. Rather than having our identity shaped by the world around us, our sense of self is now morphed into union with I AM: "And not being fashioned according to the world, but rather being morphed in our identity by the complete change of our mind that we may have experiential evidence of the good, and pleasing, and complete purpose of God."[16]

As we stand in agreement with our true I AM, the power of the whole universe begins to work in us, through us, and for us! Abiding in the Now, by inner identification with I AM, we become fully conscious. We become stereo conscious—conscious of *what* we are in union with *who* we are. Our humanity becomes subject to and melded with our divinity. We become aware of our oneness with the Universal, the I AM within whom "we all live and move and have our being."[17]

In recognizing that we are the dwelling place of the infinite "Be-er," we begin to see all things within the environment of I AM. He is the atmosphere within which "all things exist and consist."[18] We are one with Him: "And you, who in the past were alienated from and at war with God in your minds through evil works, He has now made *one*."[19] In this light of oneness, we are able to see through our present temporal situation. Even though our thinker may not see it as good, yet in our Knower we see through to the Real, to the substance of spirit, which is eternal. Seeing through allows the Presence of I AM to permeate every circumstance we encounter, thereby empowering us to triumph in all situations. God in us, making Himself known to us and through us, bears witness of Himself to the world: "You shall be witness of Me."[20]

Our one sacred trust, therefore, is to abide in conscious union with the One. It is to our great benefit to stay present. Our freedom and our salvation stem from living in the Now. Jesus said, "*Abide in Me*, as I abide in you, and fruitfulness will happen naturally."[21] To stand in Presence is to accept the Now without rejecting it by own judgment, without reacting to it by trying to change it. To be present in the moment is to live beyond the confines of time and space while in our temporal body. By surrendering the thoughts of our mind to our true I AM within, we choose Life as opposed to living in death. As we abide in Presence, our thinker, now brought under our Knower, is able to receive words of instruction, guidance, and wisdom from our true Center. We thus live in abundant life, a life that has no beginning, no end and no limits. We enter into eternity, here and now! "All things are possible to those who believe into I AM."[22]

As the fire teaches us to disassociate our sense of self from our compulsive thinking, we become increasingly conscious of who we really are in this moment! This is the practice of being: "Beloved, *now* we *are* the sons of God although it is not yet apparent what we shall be, however we know that when He is fully recognized we shall be like Him for we shall gaze at Him as He truly is."[23] Our baptism in the fire is the training program that entitles us to step into our true identity as I AM and confess that "As I AM *is*, so are we in this world."[24] We awaken to the realization that "there is only one God, the Father, out from whom all things are created and we exist within Him; and one Lord Jesus Christ, through whom all things exist, and we exist because of Him."[25]

This in no way implies that we can become Almighty God in our own right. No finite human can ever become the infinite God. Yet the one and only self-sustaining Being can and does manifest Himself in human form—as human beings. It is His design and His delight to do so, *in us—as us*! It is our inheritance to abide in Him *as our* I AM, for He is One, and He is All!

Notes

1   Eph. 1:14, italics added
2   John 1:4
3   Rom. 8:28
4   2 Cor. 4:17
5   Gal. 3:27; 1 Cor. 2:16
6   2 Cor. 12:9,10, paraphrase
7   Gal. 2:20, paraphrase
8   Rom. 12:1, paraphrase
9   1 Thess. 5:18, italics added
10   Heb. 13:15, italics added
11   Col. 1:27
12   John 4:4, paraphrase
13   James 4:72
14   Tim. 2:25, italics added
15   Matt. 5:39
16   Rom. 12:2, paraphrase
17   Acts 17:28
18   Col. 1:16,17
19   Col. 1:21, italics added
20   Acts 1:8, italics added
21   John 15:5, paraphrase
22   Mark 9:23
23   1 John 3:2, italics added
24   1 John 4:17, paraphrase
25   1 Cor. 8:6

Chapter 13

The Key to the Kingdom

As our mind is renewed in the fire, a major paradigm shift begins to occur in regard to how we derive our sense of self. This shift is due to a subtle transfer of allegiance from intellectual thought to inner spirit knowing. The meager diet of rational concepts we have subsisted on in the past no longer satisfies our inner cravings. Now that the smell of the real food has aroused our hunger, the pictures in the menu no longer hold our interest. We begin to develop an appetite for genuine encounter with spiritual reality and thus naturally begin to lose confidence in our thinker and its ability to tell us who we are.

In due course, as we gain personal experience of spiritual reality, our confidence becomes firmly rooted in our Knower. Under the tutelage of our Knower, our thinker finds its intended function, and as a result we discover our identity being transformed from *I am* to I AM! This shift in our identity in no way minimizes our human nature but, on the contrary, enhances our uniqueness as human beings. In much the same way, light transforms the darkness of materiality; our humanity is transformed by yielding to our divinity. Even as light uses darkness as a medium by which to reveal its concealed splendor, our humanity becomes the stage on which the invisible attributes of the infinite God are displayed to the physical world around us. In regard to our identity therefore, we literally become someone we formerly could not have imagined.[1] Rather than losing our uniqueness, with I AM as our identity, our individuality blossoms into its true function and glorious potential.

Although we forever remain created human beings by nature, we are now enabled to identify our being human with its true source. The fire literally metamorphoses our sense of self into a whole new person. We become a new creation—a new creature in Christ. We awaken to the reality that we are a corporate being![2] This new sense of self is rooted in inner knowing rather than founded on intellectual thinking. In scripture, the apostle Paul distinguishes between rational knowledge and inner knowing by his use of different Greek words. Unfortunately the distinct meanings of these words are lost in English, as they are often translated with the same verb *to know*. The word *eido* means "to perceive with the senses or to get intellectual knowledge of a fact." The word *ginosko* has a similar meaning. It means "to learn, to get knowledge of, to perceive, and to be aware"; whereas his use of the word *epiginosko* carries an entirely different meaning. *Epiginosko* means "to know upon a mark, to become thoroughly acquainted with, or to know accurately and fully." In other words, *epiginosis* refers to absolute knowledge, *gnosis* refers to "experiential knowledge learned as a science," while *eido* simply means "to get an intellectual grasp of information with the senses."

It is very interesting to note that the word *eidolon* (which stems from *eido*) is the Greek word for *idol*. *Eidolon* literally means "a mental image or a phantom of the mind." *Eidololatreia* is the Greek word for *idolatry*. The point is our worship of a false god takes place in the mind, setting our desires on mental images. Examples of the above terms for knowing as used in scripture are as follows:

- "Therefore we are always confident, *knowing* [eido] that, while we are at home in the body, we are absent from the Lord."[3]
- "For we *know in part* [ginosko], and we prophesy from a portion. But when we mature our immaturity is displaced.

When I was an infant, I spoke like an immature person, I had childish opinions and sentiments, I reasoned like a simple minded person: but when I became a man, my immaturity vanished. For now we look into a mirror with obscurity; but then face to face: now *I know in part* [ginosko]; but then *I shall know* [epiginosko] even as *I am* also *known* [epiginosko]."[4]

Without this inner shift of confidence from intellectual knowledge [thinking] to knowing, it is impossible to walk in the kingdom of heaven. In order to enter and abide in the kingdom of heaven, it is imperative we know who we are. Jesus questioned His followers in regard to His own identity in order to reveal their own inner allegiance, "Who do you say that I am?"[5] At one point, Peter demonstrated that he truly knew the real identity of Jesus when he said, "You are the Christ, the Son of the living God."[6] Jesus responded to this revelation with a profound statement:

> "You are blessed Peter, because flesh and blood did not reveal this to you, but my Father who is in heaven [revealed this knowledge]. You are *Petros* [a rock] but upon this *petra* [bedrock] I will build my church and the gates of hell will not stand up against it. And [by this] I will give you the key to the Kingdom of Heaven, so whatever you shall bind upon the earth shall come to pass, having been bound in heaven, and whatever you shall loose upon the earth shall come to pass, having been loosed in the heavens."[7]

With a careful study of the verb tenses in this statement, it becomes apparent that the "binding and loosing," which is to be undertaken on earth, is accomplished on the basis of knowing (*epiginosis*) what is already bound and loosed in heaven. This *revelation knowledge* is the bedrock upon which the church is built, ensuring the corporate Body of Christ victory over the powers of hell. It is this *inner knowing* that gives us access to the kingdom of heaven.

Knowing (*epiginosis*) therefore is the key to entering and walking in the kingdom of heaven! The key is *being in the Know*—being *in* Christ "in whom are hidden all the treasures of wisdom and knowledge."[8]

Living in our Knower far surpasses walking in our thinker. Knowing is the result of trusting what has been revealed to us in the invisible realm. Knowing is revelation knowledge as opposed to outward experiential knowledge or conceptual knowledge: "Faith is the *substance* of things hoped for, the *evidence* of things which are invisible."[9] Knowing has its roots in the invisible realm, that permanent universe that is the foundation and infrastructure of the visible realm. The visible world is merely the temporary superstructure by which the invisible realm is manifested materially. Compared to the substantiality of the invisible realm, the visible universe is merely a shadow. Even as the physical realm is less substantial than the unseen world of spirit, so also thinking is inferior to and subordinate to knowing.

If we walk according to our thinking, we are bound by the parameters of the material universe. But as we learn to walk according to our knowing, we are released from the limitations of the physical realm and set free to walk in the resources of the limitless realm of spirit. Inner seeing, trusting, and knowing are developmental expressions of faith. Knowing is the consequence of having encountered the power of the kingdom of heaven experientially.

As a result of our conception from above, we are able to see into the invisible, and as we learn to trust in that sight, we then begin to know, i.e., we learn to walk by faith. When we know something in the spirit world, we then have the authority and the power to "call" that inner sight into manifestation in the material realm. We have the key to the kingdom of heaven: "All things are possible to him who believes [entrusts]."[10] If we are limited merely to the thoughts and opinions of our own mind, we are not only subject to the natural laws of the physical universe but are also blind to the real world of spirit.

Our ability to think and reason develops and matures through personal experience. Knowing is also a proficiency that comes through practice. This is not to say that our capacity to know increases, any more than our IQ could increase, but rather we learn to *walk* in our knowing in much the same way we learn to walk in our thinking, through experience. Even as our mental capacities must be exercised in order to become proficient, so likewise our faculty of knowing is trained by experience in the unseen realm. Scripture refers to this process as follows: "Solid nourishment belongs to those who are mature, who by reason of exercise have their senses [literally, inner organ of perception] trained to discern between that which is worthy and that which is worthless."[11]

We were born with a given capacity to think—with a given IQ. We are born again in spirit with a gifted measure of knowing: "God has dealt to every man the measure of faith."[12] Naturally we are born into the visible world with an ability to behold the material world. In like manner, we are reborn into the spiritual realm with a corresponding capacity to perceive the invisible world. Rational understanding and intellectual comprehension are the outcomes of observing and studying material things. So likewise, knowing is the result of beholding the unseen things of the spirit realm. As with outward sight, we believe what we see inwardly, and we learn to know what we believe as we experience these unseen realities on an ongoing basis. Walking by faith is a proficiency we must learn. We learn to walk according to knowing rather than by rational thought. "We walk by faith not by sight."[13] Our baptism of repentance in the fire is the school in which we learn to walk by knowing in the kingdom of heaven.

Scripture declares that knowing is a faculty of spirit, not a function of the mind. As quoted earlier, "It is spirit that *knows* the thoughts of a man."[14] Spirit knows the thoughts; the mind merely thinks those thoughts. We can quite safely say that the mind cannot know anything on its own as far as spirit realities are concerned. It is for this reason that the mind must be brought under the spirit, to be taught by the spirit, rather than allowed to rule over spirit with its relative perception. Our thinker was not designed to know the realities of the invisible world: "The rational mind cannot download spiritual realities because they seem absurd and ridiculous to natural reason. Such realities cannot be known rationally because they are divinely discerned."[15] Consequently, the sooner we learn to live consistently in our Knower, the sooner we will walk without stumbling in the unseen realm of spirit.

As long as our confidence is rooted in our own thinking, we will find ourselves dependent upon and locked into the material realm. We literally become hooked to material things. In the true sense of the word, we are materialistic, or as scripture states, "We are yet carnal."[16] In this state of spiritual unconsciousness, our life *does* "consist in the abundance of things which we possess,"[17] simply because we do not behold the invisible world in which our life is truly constituted.

The scripture says, "Lean not on your own understanding [your own thoughts, your own mind] but in all your ways *acknowledge* God and He will direct your paths."[18] The Hebrew word for *acknowledge* literally means "to ascertain by seeing." As we continue to look into the spirit realm, our confidence in our own rational understanding begins to wane, and outward things lose their addictive appeal. When we have learned to walk in the spirit, in our knower, the visible world no longer dictates our existence because our rational confidence is undermined.

The fact is we cannot walk in our thinker and our Knower simultaneously. In whatever degree we walk in our thinker, to that very degree we limit our confidence in our Knower: "No man can serve two masters [two opposing paradigms]. You cannot serve God and mammon."[19] The word *mammon* is a Chaldean word which means "confidence that comes from wealth," i.e., self-confidence. To the degree that we lose confidence in our thinker, in the same measure we gain confidence in our Knower. This transfer in confidence occurs as the thinker is brought under the Knower. Rather than an overlord, the thinker becomes an obedient servant of the Knower: "The desire of the natural mind is set against spirit and spirit sets its desire against the natural mind. These are set in opposition to each other so we cannot do what we decide [with our mind]."[20] Although we walk in both the natural and the spiritual realms, we can only be ruled by one. Although totally integrated these two paradigms are mutually exclusive in their modus operandi.

We may not have recognized that self-confidence (confidence in our own mind) is unbelief in God, but Jesus made this clear when He said, "He who is not with Me is against Me, and he who does not gather with Me scatters abroad."[21] To whatever degree we think we can do something from a sense of own self, to that same degree we live in opposition to spirit, i.e., we quench the indwelling Holy Spirit of I AM.[22] But as we are awakened into knowing and our confidence shifts from outward shadows to inward substance, we find ourselves empowered to walk in the reality of the kingdom of heaven in the midst: "We know even as we are known."[23] Simply put, we trust God Himself within as our true Center instead of the judgments of our own mind. Knowing empowers us to walk in our inheritance, granting us access to the kingdom of heaven on earth!

Notes

1   1 Cor. 2:9

2   2 Cor. 5:17

3   2 Cor. 5:6, italics added

4   1 Cor. 13:9-12, italics added

5   Matt. 16:15

6   Matt. 16:16

7   Matt. 16:17-19, italics added

8   Col. 2:3

9   Heb. 11:1, italics added

10   Mark 9:23

11   Heb. 5:14

12   Rom. 12:3

13   2 Cor. 5:7

14   1 Cor. 2:11, italics added

15   1 Cor. 2:14, paraphrase

16   1 Cor. 3:3

17 Luke 12:15
18 Prov. 3:5,6, italics added
19 Matt. 6:24
20 Gal. 5:17
21 Matt. 12:30
22 1 Thess. 5:19
23 1 Cor. 13:12

Chapter 14

The Power of Knowing

Although the thinker cannot initially appreciate its own incompetence when weighed against inner knowing, once we step over into our Knower, this fact will become abundantly obvious. In contrast to our Knower, our thinker has no power at all because it is dependent on spirit to interpret its whole sense of awareness. For the spirit "knows all things" in an absolute or universal sense whereas the mind can only ever consider anything in relative terms, i.e., in relationship to something else. For example, rationally we only know hard in relation to soft, cold in relation to hot, up in relation to down, sweet in relation to sour, etc. The Knower, on the other hand, understands reality from an absolute perspective.

There are many scriptures that illustrate the power of knowing, but none are as apparent as the scriptures that refer to the person of Christ Jesus. Although scripture declares that Jesus was perfect in every way,[1] it is evident from what He said about Himself in scripture that He had no confidence in Himself whatsoever. He did not trust His own mind. He freely admitted this of Himself:

- "I can of My own self [my humanity] do *nothing*, I judge, and My judgment is just; because I seek not My own desire, but the will of the Father who has sent Me."[2]
- "The Son can do *nothing* of Himself, except what He sees the Father do."[3]
- "The words that I speak unto you I speak not of Myself, but the Father who indwells Me, He does the works."[4]
- "For I have not spoken of Myself; the Father who sent Me has Himself given Me commandment what to say and what to speak."[5]
- "My teaching is not Mine, but His who sent Me."[6]

It was this inner knowing that enabled Jesus to walk in the power of the unseen world where He saw His Father at work. He walked in an inner confidence that never wavered, even in life-threatening circumstances:.

- "Jesus, *knowing* that the Father had given all things into His hands, and [*knowing*] that He had come from God, and [*knowing*] He was going to God, arose from supper, took off His robe, wrapped a cloth around Himself and with water began to wash and wipe the disciples feet."[7]
- "Jesus therefore, *knowing* all things that should come upon Him, went forth, and said unto them: Who do you seek?"[8]
- "After this, Jesus *knowing* that all things were now accomplished, that the scripture might be fulfilled, said, I thirst."[9]

It is this inner knowing that constitutes our connection to God. Knowing allows us to experience the power of God that operates in the kingdom of heaven: "And Jesus, immediately *knowing* in Himself that virtue had gone out of Him, turned around in the crowd, and said: 'Who touched My clothes?' But the woman fearing and trembling, *knowing* what was done in her, came and fell down before Him, and told Him all the truth."[10]

Knowing unhooks us from our false identity and cancels the power of sin: "*Knowing* this, that our old self [our former I am] is put to death in union together with I AM, that the body of sin [our false identity] might be rendered powerless, that from now on we should not be enslaved to sin [the virus that promotes our false ID]. For he who is dead is freed from sin."[11]

It is knowing that delivers us from the fear of evil by empowering us to live in a world that has no perception of evil in it: "We *know* that *all things* work together for *good* for those who love God, who are called according to His purpose. Who or what shall separate us from the love of Christ? Indeed, I am convinced [*I know*] that . . . nothing or no one . . . shall be able to separate us from the love of God, which is in Christ Jesus our Lord."[12] That which the thinker perceives as evil, the Knower sees as God working for good.

This same knowing is what delivers us from the fear of death and sets us free to participate in the resurrection life of Jesus in us here and now:

> *Now* since we *are* dead with Christ, we believe that we shall *now* also live in union with Him: *knowing* that Christ having been raised from the dead can die no more; death has no more power over Him. For His death was a one time death to sin, but His life *now* is a perpetual life which He is living to God. Even so *reckon yourselves as* [consider to the point of *knowing* that you are] dead to sin, but living to God *in* Christ Jesus.[13]

This scripture defines true repentance: seeing Christ within as our true Self, knowing ourselves to be alive to God in His resurrected life, having died to sin in His death.

It is knowing that awakens us from the dream of death into the resurrection life of Jesus in the Now: "And *knowing* the time, that now *it is high time* to awake out of sleep: for now is our salvation nearer than when we believed."[14]

Knowing is what enables us to endure our baptism in the fire with expectation:

- "And not only so, but we glory in tribulations also, *knowing* that tribulation produces patience, and patience, experience, and experience, hope; and hope makes us not ashamed, because the love of God is shed abroad in our hearts by the Holy Spirit who is given unto us."[15]
- "And our hope of you is steadfast, *knowing,* that as you are partakers of the sufferings, so also you shall be of the consolation."[16]

It is significant to note that it is not knowledge about God that saves us, but personally knowing God Himself gives us the assurance that we are already walking in eternal life: "And this is life eternal, that they might *know* You the only true God and Jesus Christ whom You have sent."[17] In other words, knowledge can never save us—not even scripture knowledge. Knowledge can only ever lead us to salvation. Salvation can only ever be experienced by knowing (relating personally to) God Himself in the Present Moment, not by holding to doctrines about God. Salvation is only in the Now—only in Christ! Knowing is always now.

We know in spirit. Spirit is the knower. Knowing is a function of spirit. Our Knower is simply *Christ in us, as us* by the power of His Holy Spirit! Christ Himself is our new man by whom we walk in the kingdom of heaven here and now! The following scriptures bear witness to the fact that Christ Jesus is our real I AM, our true identity:

- "In Him we *know* that we remain in Him, and He in us, because He has given us of His Spirit."[18]

- "And In Him we *know* that He abides in us, by the Spirit which He has given us."[19]
- "In Him we *know* that we are of the truth, and shall assure our hearts before Him. For if our heart condemns us, I AM is greater than our heart, and *knows* all things."[20]
- "We are of God, he who *knows* God listens to us; he that is not of God does not pay attention to us. In Him we *know* the spirit of truth, and the spirit of error."[21]
- "We *know* that we have passed from death unto life, because we love the brethren. We *know* that, when He shall appear, we shall be like Him; for we shall see Him as He IS."[22]
- "In Him we *know* that we are in Him. Anyone who says he abides in Him will also walk even as He walked."[23]
- "And we *know* that the Son of God is present, and has given us an understanding, that we may *know* Him who is truth, and we are in Him who is truth, even in His Son Jesus Christ. This is the true I AM, and eternal life."[24]
- "In Him we *know* that we *know* Him."[25]

The only way that we can know that we know, rather than merely think we know, is in Him—in our real Self. We cannot know anything beyond the natural realm unless we abide in our Knower. If we do not stay present in our Knower, we fall asleep into spiritual unconsciousness. The thinker cannot know anything spiritual, except as information. As long as we live in our thinker, under the domination of our mind, we know nothing as it should be known: "And if any man *thinks he knows* any thing, he *knows nothing* yet as he ought to know."[26] When we live in our thinker, we are literally unconscious, for consciousness is a function of spirit. True human consciousness therefore is the fruit of living in our Knower—surrendering our thinker to our Knower.

These are the questions confronting each of us here:

- Have we been awakened into knowing?

- Can we discern between soul and spirit, between thinking and knowing?
- Are we practiced in observing our thoughts and judging them or are we subject to the judgment of our own thoughts?
- Do we walk in the spirit or in the flesh?
- Are we learning to walk in our Knower?
- Do we know what it means to surrender our thinker to our knower?
- Do we know who we are?
- Do we know in our Knower?
- Do we know that we know or are we merely thinking we know?

Notes

1   Heb. 2:10
2   John 5:30, italics added
3   John 5:19, italics added
4   John 14:10
5   John 12:49
6   John 7:16
7   John 13:3,4, italics added
8   John 18:4, italics added
9   John 19:28, italics added
10 Mark 5:30, italics added
11 Rom. 6:6,7, italics added
12 Rom. 8:28,35,38,39, italics added
13 Rom. 6:8-11, italics added
14 Rom. 13:11, italics added
15 Rom. 5:3-5, italics added
16 2 Cor. 1:7, italics added
17 John 17:3, italics added
18 1 John 4:13, italics added
19 1 John 3:24b, italics added

20 1 John 3:19,20, italics added
21 1 John 4:6, italics added
22 1 John 3:14, italics added
23 1 John 2:5b,6, italics added
24 1 John 5:20, paraphrase
25 1 John 2:3, italics added
26 1 Cor. 8:2, italics added

Chapter 15

Breathing

If these conclusions regarding our identity are true, how should we then live? If our salvation, our freedom from enslavement to a false identity, is to live in absolute surrender to God-in-us, with "every thought being brought captive to I AM's compliance,"[1] what does this total surrender look like? How are we to realistically participate in the birthing process that God is generating in the human race? Are there any practical ways in which we can cooperate? In other words, how do we refrain from resisting what God-in-us is determining to accomplish through us individually and corporately?

The obvious thing we can do is to acknowledge that we have been asleep since birth, i.e., that we have been spiritually unconscious. Beyond this, we begin by simply agreeing with God that we have "missed the mark, and fallen short of God's indwelling glory."[2] We have missed our true I AM by unconsciously adhering to a false sense of independent self. It is to our great advantage to admit that we have sinned,[3] i.e., allowed SIN (Satan's Incarnate Nature) to manifest through us. By identifying with a counterfeit *I am*, we have granted Satan and his kingdom of darkness undisputed access to our humanity to propagate his corrupt nature through us. In this we have not only grieved the indwelling Spirit of Christ but we may have resisted the Spirit's activity to the point of quenching Him.[4] But now, as the desire for our lost divinity is aroused within us, we recognize the power of the Holy Spirit who is awakening us into I AM's immanent presence. By attentively listening to His prompting within, we give place to I AM's passionate longing for our affections: "You will seek Me and find Me, when you search for Me with all your heart."[5]

Aside from these elementary essentials, it is primarily a matter of standing and walking in what is, without resistance. In fact, much of what we experience on a moment-by-moment basis can assist in this radical exchange that is revolutionizing our identity from *I am* to I AM, when we consider it consciously. Let's return to our breathing exercise from chapter 2. This exercise of momentarily observing your breath is so simple; you may be tempted to think it is of little or no consequence. However, take a moment now to be still. Close your eyes and contemplate your breath. As you turn your attention inward, becoming aware of your chest and abdomen rising and falling with each breath, stand back behind your thoughts and feelings and begin to observe them. As you enter fully into this capacity of observer, you will become conscious of the surrounding "space" in which your breathing is taking place. Identify with this inner space, within which everything exists in the moment. Recognize this space as a presence, as an infinite person, and consider the fact that you are one with this person. For truly, as it is written, "In Him, the Almighty God, who Himself grants to all life and breath and all good things, we all live and move and have our being."[6]

As we become more fully conscious in Him, we will begin to realize that breathing isn't something we do, but rather it is something that is happening to us—something that is being done for us. Our mind has always tried to own this activity. In fact, we have been taught that it is an activity of our subconscious mind. But the instant we become truly aware of our innermost Being, our mind is arrested in its delusion. At that moment, the mind stops functioning independently of the spirit.

—

If only for a split second, our thinker ceases to form its own opinions and judgments and simply takes its legitimate place in subordination to our Knower—to our true Self. It is at moments like this that we actually awaken from the mind dream we were born into and become stereo-conscious of God-in-us and ourselves-in-God.

Our breath can be one of the most powerful reminders of God's immediate presence—when we see it for what it is. We have unconsciously owned our breath by thinking of our breathing as something we do subconsciously with our mind. Yet if we thought it through, we would ultimately recognize that breathing is not a task performed by the mind. Breathing comes from a much deeper level of consciousness than mind activity.

As repentance finds a place in us, we eventually realize that our breath is not really ours at all, but God's Spirit in us, as scripture clearly states, "If He made *His* Spirit come back to Him, taking *His* breath unto Himself again all flesh would come to an end together, and man would go back to the dust."[7] If our breath truly is "God's breath" in us, then could it not just as well be God Himself in us breathing? Is not this what the apostle Paul meant when he said, "for it is God working in you both to will and to do"?[8] And is this not why he urges us to "work out our own salvation with fear and trembling,"[9]—lest we forget who we really are?

The independent mind is accustomed to usurping control over every facet of our lives. It relentlessly attempts to steal the present moment from us by instantly forming mental concepts and rational ideas about our experience of the moment. Because our mind is so rarely called into question or held in check, our thoughts have become completely dominant. Our mind has become a law unto itself. Our thinker literally becomes our god—evaluating, manipulating, arbitrating, and controlling absolutely everything we experience. We are so used to letting our mind rule us that we are completely unconscious that it is happening and that we have become slaves of our thoughts. We have fallen so far over into our mind that we don't even question that our thoughts are not who we are. We unconsciously think that we are doing the thinking when, in fact, our thinking is happening to us. Unbeknown to us, we have become captives of our own minds. Without even being aware of it, very often our minds are completely under the domination of the spirit of the cosmos, the god of this world.

The truth is most of the time we are literally unconscious inside our mind. We act and react spontaneously, without knowing why. Like a cork in the rapids, we are caught in the incessant stream of thoughts that flow relentlessly through our mind. *Who we really are* is literally held captive to *who we think we are*. Our true Self is kept locked away in a closet behind the pseudo identity our mind has created. Because our whole sense of self is so completely derived from our thoughts, we have become totally oblivious to our true Center. In a very real sense, we are asleep in a dreamworld, all the while dreaming that we are awake in what we imagine is the real world outside of us. Until we are awakened into knowing, it never occurs to us that the more substantial world is within, in spirit and truth, not outward in materiality and form.

Perhaps by this point, you are feeling somewhat dubious about the direction this book is taking. Possibly at the root of your uneasiness is the nagging question: why would the Creator give us a mind and then expect us not to exercise it? Maybe what you've been hearing is that we are to put our mind on the shelf or maybe even trash our mind and live happily ever after without our mind. If this is what you are hearing, be assured this is the furthest thing from what is being advocated.

It isn't that our mind should not be engaged. The use of our rational mind is essential to our life as human beings on planet Earth. Our thinker is designed to link our Knower to the physical realm. But our thinker is not our true Self and therefore has no right or ability to rule over our being, enslaving us to a false I am—a false god. Our mind was designed to be the servant of our true I AM, not the master! Our thoughts do not constitute who we really are. Our true identity is beyond our mind, beyond our thoughts, beyond even our imagination! Our real identity is rooted in God Himself, for we are God's offspring![10]

As we have noted earlier, there are numerous scriptures that clearly associate our breath with the presence of God's Spirit. In fact, scripture refers to our breath synonymously with the indwelling Spirit of God:

- "The Spirit of God hath made me, and the breath of the Almighty has given me life."[11]
- "If Your face is veiled, they are troubled; when You take away their breath, they come to an end, and go back to the dust. If You send out Your Spirit, they are given life."[12]

This is the reason for suggesting that we contemplate our breathing. If our breath is simply the Spirit of God in us giving us life, then it naturally follows that to become conscious of our breathing for what it really is, is in a very real sense to become aware of God's presence in us, in the present moment.

The mind automatically conceives of life and breath as something God dispenses. In our separation thinking, we naturally think of life and breath as attributes or "commodities" that God gives separately of Himself. But this is not what the scriptures declare. It is plainly stated, "He *Himself* gives life and breath to all."[13] Meditate on this for as long as it takes for your mind to submit to the full reality of it, until every thought surrenders to the truth of what these scriptures declare. Is it possible to separate life from breath? Can we have life without breath or breath without life? Are not life and breath one and the same? If the Spirit of God is our life and breath, then life is simply one of the ways the Spirit of God manifests Himself in living things. This is the same as to say He Himself is our breath in us. Yes! He is literally our breathing!

Several times in the Gospels, Jesus declared, "I am . . . *the life.*"[14] It should be carefully noted here that Jesus did not claim to *have* life, but rather He professed to *be* life. There is an immeasurable distinction between *having* something and *being* something. If the Spirit of God is life, then it follows just as surely that the Spirit of God Himself is our life, and our breath. As much as the rational mind struggles with this and would like to conceive of these attributes as separate from God, life and breath cannot be separated from the presence and person of the Holy Spirit, any more than sunlight can be separated from the sun. Is it possible to have sunlight without the sun, or the sun without sunlight? It is equally impossible to have life or breath without the Holy Spirit Himself being present as our life and breath! The reason the mind struggles with this is because it does not want to relinquish its assumed godhood to the indwelling presence of I AM. In other words, the powers of darkness that have incarnated themselves within man's identity do not want to lose their seat of government over the human soul.

How then do we discover this awareness of God's Spirit and breath in us? By now the answer is obvious but bears repeating once more. It is by the process of repentance, the exchange of our mind, that we are enabled to escape our thinker and step into our Knower. The mind, in its unruly thinking, must be brought under the Knower, made subject to Christ Himself in us—our I AM. By acquiescing to, and cooperating with, the presence of God in this process of inner transformation, we awaken into the true consciousness of Being. In the fire, through the power of the Holy Spirit of Christ within, we literally wake up to who we really are, to our true identity. As the mind is trained to stand in attentive hearkening to the Spirit within, we are exercised in the practice of being.[15] Although this baptism of repentance may seem entirely foreign to the thinker, it is the most natural thing in the world. In fact, it's more natural than natural—it is super-natural!

Notes

1   2 Cor. 10:5

2   Rom. 3:23

3   1 John 1:8
4   Eph. 4:20, 1 Thes. 5:19
5   Jer. 29:13
6   Acts 17:25,28
7   Job 34:14, 15, italics added
8   Phil. 2:13
9   Phil. 2:12
10 Acts 17:28
11 Job 33:4
12 Ps. 104:29,30
13 Acts 17:25, italics added
14 John 11:25, 14:6, italics added
15 Heb. 5:14

Chapter 16

Love is ALL

In our mistaken identity, we invariably find ourselves living with a vague sense of lack that operates just below the conscious level of our mind. Although we have no comprehension of where this ambivalence stems from, we sense that somehow, somewhere, we have lost something profoundly essential. At an instinctive level of awareness, we can't let go of the haunting feeling that we are coping with a significant deficit. Although we are driven by this innate, gnawing impulse to achieve, to acquire, and to become, we are never quite sure what it is we are searching for, or why.

In our unconscious state of compulsive thinking, it perpetually escapes our awareness that our fundamental need is simply to *be*—to be fully conscious, to be aware of who we are, to abide in I AM. To the rational mind, this makes no sense at all because the mind is completely occupied with thinking and doing in a frantic attempt to establish and maintain our false sense of self. *Being*, as an end in itself, is perceived by the mind to be a total waste of time. Nonetheless, our mind-bound identity can offer us no lasting solution to the insanity that overcomes us from within, which moves us to want, to covet, to resent, to hate, and even to kill each other in order to acquire and protect what we deem are our just desserts.

This perpetual state of *unknowing* is, without doubt, the most distressing symptom of living with a false identity. It is this incognizance, felt within as fear and greed, which compels us to do those things we never imagined we could do. We are astounded, and even terrorized, by the propensity to depravity we find inherent within our humanity. As a human race, we are deeply troubled by this. Why do we hate each other to the point of exterminating our own species? Why have we murdered millions of humans just like ourselves? Where does this abject lack of love for our own humanity stem from?

In our self-centered state of independence, we imagine we know what we need, but our false identity repeatedly deceives us, identifying our lack as this thing or that thing. Yet *no-thing* ever seems to quench the insatiable thirst of our soul life. The truth is, our mind cannot figure out what we need. In fact, our thinker has no idea what we crave at the deepest level of consciousness. However, scripture asserts that we will forfeit everything for our being: "All that a man has he will give in exchange for his life [for his being]."[1] The fact that we are willing to give up everything in exchange for *being* should tell us that our humanity is essentially an intense desire for *being*. Is not our insatiable need for the next breath sufficient evidence that we crave *being* more than anything else? In fact, our human life is, by its very nature, a desire for I AM. We *are* in essence a hunger and a thirst for the infinite reality of Being—the being of Almighty God. In all truth, our humanity was birthed out of the infinite being of God, as a desire for Himself alone.

Yet, even though by the very nature of our human existence, we are designed for intimate union relationship with the infinite nature of our Eternal Father, the rational mind cannot, by its endless reasoning, discern what that infinite nature is. In our false identity, it escapes us completely that the nature of this Being who gave birth to our humanity is completely unknown to us. Who is this inconceivable Being we refer to as God? What is God like? What is God's irreducible essence? What are God's incomprehensible attributes? On these crucial issues, the thinker falters and is found wanting for it cannot move past the limits of its self-generated speculation. The thinker cannot scrutinize the being of God anymore than darkness can analyze light.

Just as it is light alone that can give birth to sight, it is the Light of I AM alone who can reveal the true nature of His own being to the blindness of our human soul. Although it is His delight to constantly reveal Himself, the soul is often too busy with its own thoughts to listen inwardly to hear that I AM is ceaselessly saying, "I AM the only I AM."[2] Indeed, only when we crash and burn does our mind come to the end of its own reasoning and begin to listen beyond its own thoughts. Hence the necessity for the fire of our baptism, that we might be brought to the knowing of I AM within.

As our minds learn to listen within, we begin to hear and see that Being, at its very root, is a consuming passion called Love—a pure, unalterable desire for all goodness. God *is* Love. Love is the unchangeable determination for all goodness and blessing. Our mind cannot tell us this by its reasoning. Indeed, it is by revelation alone that the soul can receive such knowledge. This inner revelation is the bedrock of all intimate relationship with God. I AM must show us the truth of His being within! No one can show another the Truth of Being. It is impossible simply because the Truth is an infinite person abiding at the core of our conscious existence. Can one person explain to another the essence and nature of light? Yet, in an instant, light can explain itself fully to the mind that is open to receive such insight. In the same way, Truth alone can reveal Himself in a knowable way.

This indwelling person, the I AM, "came forth"[3] in outward form as the man Jesus to reveal the Father's nature. In beholding the "form of God,"[4] we have the opportunity to look into the face of Love and recognize our true I AM. Jesus the Christ came to show us the Father.[5] He came to reveal who we really are—to show us that we are the offspring of the infinite Being of Love. The essence of this being called Love is compassion, mercy, and forgiveness for SIN.

In a very literal sense, therefore, God does not *have* love to bestow on His offspring. God *is* Love: "Whoever abides in love resides in God."[6] If God is Love, then Love in essence is God. In loving us, God simply bestows Himself in the measure of our need. Yet how are we to recognize the nature of this infinite Being called Love? This divine Love is an unquenchable desire to be every creature's good. This Love cannot change. Love does not fluctuate or vary in intensity. Love is constant. Love does not twist or turn. Love simply IS. Love is boundless. Love is inescapable. Love is indestructible. Love is omnipresent. Love is unwearied patience. Love is all-knowing. Love is the one universal power that works in all things. Love is ALL! Therefore in order for God to love us as humans, God Himself must indwell our soul life, at the core of our conscious being, as the sum total of our goodness. Thus is the universal love of God.

Love is also bilateral. Love by its very nature is mutual. Love is not real unless it is reciprocal. This means God's love must be received by the human soul to be known. Love cannot be known by reason or any intellectual power. Love must be experienced inwardly to be comprehended. The rational mind can form thoughts about Love and describe with words this infinite being called Love, but the mind cannot receive or communicate this power. Love is infinite. Love is beyond the rational mind in the same way eating is beyond seeing. We cannot alleviate our hunger by looking at a restaurant menu. The only possible way our human soul can experience infinite Love is to surrender its whole being to Love in the moment, in the same way we would surrender our hungry stomachs to a full meal.

Love is not something the soul can have or possess, anymore than our lungs could possess the atmosphere around us. The human soul can only be possessed by Love as the soul surrenders itself to Love; in the same way, we surrender our lungs to the atmosphere and allow the atmosphere to possess us. Like the little bottle in the ocean that can only taste the ocean one bottle full at a time, the human soul must participate in Love moment by moment in order to know Love.

To experience Love in its true formless nature, we must surrender our soul completely to the rule and authority of Love. Otherwise, Love is merely a concept, an idea that we have locked away in our memory of a past experience. Love is now or never. Love is only experienced within that space we call the present tense or Presence because Love *is* I AM. Love cannot be transported into the past or the future. Whenever we attempt to find Love beyond or outside of Presence, Love becomes something else—something that in the end isolates us from real Love. For Love is no thing. Love is ALL.

Yet how can this be? If Love is ALL, from what source do evil and wrath arise? Evil is the offspring, which the human soul gives birth to in its denial of Love as its true Center. In our choice of independent selfhood, we prostitute ourselves to a false *I am*, giving birth to an evil offspring. Our false identity instinctively stands in resistance to our true Center. As an adversary to I AM, this false self operates in direct opposition to Love. It is only reasonable to conclude that if our created self is consciously broken off from intimate relationship with infinite Goodness residing at the core of our existence, we as created selves cannot but act out of our own created nature, which by its very nature is the want of God, the want of Love who is all goodness.[7] It is also self-evident that a want of all goodness is as much a lack of all goodness as it is evil. Thus in our blindness to the truth of I AM within, we give birth to evil in God's name! The more religious we become in the support of our false identity, the more diabolical we turn out to be. True religion is to abide in Love—to *be* Love.

The fallout of this inner resistance to the divine presence abiding within our humanity is experienced as wrath, a passion that we call the wrath of God. This wrath is not the result of our I AM becoming offended or because Love has turned against us in anger. Love is unalterable. Love, by nature, forever remains an unquenchable desire for all goodness, for our goodness. Yet the wrath we experience in our humanity is real. The reason we experience Love as wrathful is because Love is a consuming passion for all goodness. Love is that fire that burns with an unquenchable zeal, desiring eternally to purify our humanity of all that is not good, all that is not real. The only possible response that an infinite power can have to that which is set against it is to consume it with unquenchable force—a strength that we in our finiteness experience as wrathful.

Love is the only reality there is! Hence all who persist in the illusion of independent selfhood *must* suffer loss in this unquenchable fire. Thus to whatever degree we identify with our rational illusions of independence, we must suffer the pain of dis-illusionment when we enter the inescapable fire of Being. "For our God *is* [in essence] a consuming fire."[8]

With all its reasoning power, our mind is unable to tell us that we are an incarnate want of this infinite Goodness who dwells at the root of our being. It seems we have to learn this the hard way through the experience of suffering, i.e., trying to find Love in all the ways Love can never be found. But when our baptism into the fire of Love brings us to the end of our imagined "own" resources, we are awakened to the reality that, by nature of our created human souls, we are essentially a hunger for Love. It is then that we wake up to the fact that Love is the immeasurable fullness of the goodness we long for.

Thus we begin to understand that even our innate want for Love is simply a response to Love's desire for our human soul: "We love God *because* Love first loves us."[9] As human beings, we are Love's love. Love desires us in our humanness. In other words, we are loved by Love because of who Love is and because of what we are. We are loved by virtue of our humanity, our want of Love, not because we do something to merit Love! Our humanity is Love's desire, an infinite desire that is inescapable. Love has set His desire upon us, and Love cannot repent (change His mind). Love is the unalterable desire for all goodness—for our individual goodness!

Clearly then it is to our great advantage to awaken from the mind dream, to abdicate our false identity, and to identify with Love. For we must not only partake of Love in order to appease the innate cravings of our soul life, but we must also be baptized into Love to the point of saturation in order to satisfy the desire of Love for our souls. In other words, we must be fused into the being of Love—we must become one with Love. To whatever degree we fail to identify with Love as our I AM, to that same degree we inevitably experience the wrath of Love in our soul. This personal experience of wrath is due, not to any anger in God, but is the result of our own determination to maintain a false identity—a determination, which by its independent nature, opposes the unalterable will of that infinite power called Love. The measure of wrath we experience is in direct proportion to how unconscious we are of our true Self.

Identifying with Love as our true self, i.e., being Love, is our one and only source of real goodness in the daily sequence of life. If we do not live in the Now, we cannot live in Love, for Love is eternally *now*. There is no other real Love but Presence, for I AM is absolute Love, and I AM is always present: "Love is an extremely *present* help in time of need."[10] The truth is we are created to be Love in the Now—incarnations of the I AM who is Love: "In Him [in union with Him] our love is made perfect, that we may have boldness in the Day of Judgment, because as He is, so are we [now] in this world."[11] As we "put off our former identity that is corrupt due to a delusion"[12] and "put on Love as our identity"[13] (i.e., identify with our true Center), our humanity is clothed in divinity. It is for this reason the scriptures state emphatically, "Put off the old man with his practices . . . put on the new man, who is renewed in knowledge [*epiginosis*] according to the likeness of the Creator."[14] This stereo-conscious state of being *in Love* is the realization of God's holy Law: "Love fulfills the whole Law."[15]

Notes

1   Job 2:4

2   Exod. 3:14

3   John 16:27,28

4   Phil. 2:6

5   John 1:18

6   1 John 4:16
7   Matt. 19:17
8   Deut. 4:24, Heb. 12:29, italics added
9   1 John 4:19, italics added
10   Ps. 46:1, paraphrase
11   1 John 4:17
12   Eph. 4:22
13   Eph. 4:24, paraphrase
14   Col. 3:9,10
15   Rom. 13:10

Conclusion

Touching the Infinite

Have you ever stood out under a clear night sky and consciously considered the black nothingness of deep space and wondered what space really is? If space was merely nothing, as the mind would tell us, how could we be separated from anything in outer space? If, on the other hand, we truly are separated from objects in deep space, then space itself cannot be nothing but must indeed be something. But what?

The reason our mind labels deep space as *nothingness* is simply because the mind is completely "form-oriented." The rational mind inevitably focuses on objects and content, which is all it can conceive of, because that is what it was designed for. Therefore, all we ever observe with our rational mind when we look up at the night sky is the moon, the planets, the stars, or some formation of objects, which monopolize our attention. Our mind has no category under which to classify the infinite expanse of space. Therefore, we don't see space because to the thinker, it is not a thing. It is no-thing, and the mind can only see things: objects with form and shape.

The same is true of the vast blue dome we call the daylight sky. Whenever we look at the sky, we are rarely even conscious of the infinite blue expanse above us because our outward eyes, which are agents of the rational mind, automatically gravitate toward objects in the sky: the passing airplane, the fluffy clouds, or the profusion of insect and birdlife.

But has it ever occurred to you that deep space and the blue atmosphere above us more accurately portray the infinite being of God than any object within them? Is not this vast outward expanse more closely representative of that inner space we refer to as Presence than any substance or form our mind can conceive of? Does not every thing exist *within* God? The scriptures declare, "For *within* Him *all things* were made, in heaven and on earth, *things seen* and *things unseen,* authorities, lords, rulers, and powers; *all things* were made through Him and into Him; He is prior to *all things,* and *within* Him *all things* have being."[1] Do the scriptures not explicitly state that all living creatures "live and move and have their being *in* God?"[2] In other words, God is the space in which everything exists and consists.

If this is true, how often do you ponder the infinite reality of the blue sky during the day or reflect on the dark expanse of outer space at night in light of God's infinite being? Even though your thinker does not know how to download this infinite reality called outer space, anymore than your mind can receive the things of the Spirit of God, these reflections are true food and real drink to your Knower. So next time you consciously take a breath, take a deep breath of blue. Breathe in the infinite expanse around you and within you! In other words, as you breathe, identify with this vast expanse with which you are one in essence. Know at a fundamental level of consciousness that you are *one* with God, who is ALL in all. This was the heart cry of Jesus when He prayed, "That they all may be ONE; as You, Father, are in Me, and I in You, that they also may be ONE in Us."[3] In this same prayer He reveals that to be conscious of this Oneness is life eternal."[4]

This absolute identification with His I AM-ness is reflected in Christ's teaching about eating His Body: "Except you eat the flesh of the Son of man, and drink His blood, you have no life in you. Whoever eats Me, even he shall live by Me."[5] Such radical identification goes far beyond ingesting the material elements with which the Christian religion celebrates the Eucharist. Jesus was referring to an assimilation of His I AM-ness at a level of consciousness that supersedes anything the mind is capable of conceiving. He was talking about spirit oneness: "Whoever is joined to the I AM is ONE spirit."[6]

This inner conscious fusion is clearly symbolized, not only in our eating, but also in our breathing. So whenever you find yourself falling into the unconscious states of stress, anxiety, or frustration, touch the infinite by taking a deep breath of infinite space. As your breath is literally being carried to each cell in your body, envision your whole being saturated with the inner atmosphere that is God. Realize that the infinite expanse around you is constantly reminding you of the infinite being of God within you, who is awakening you into the Presence of Oneness.

Make a practice of this every time it comes to you. Breathe in the universal presence of Being and breathe out the stress and anxiety of unconsciousness. This is the essence of what it means to pray. Prayer is simply breathing in the mind of God while breathing out the toxic waste of our own thoughts that do not reflect God's "ALL-ness." Waste products are inevitable in the assimilation process of our physical body, and we need good elimination to keep us healthy. The same is true spiritually. If we fail to inhale the rarefied atmosphere of Presence or forget to exhale the delusional thought processes of our own mind, we end up emotionally, mentally, and spiritually toxic and physically diseased. This is true religion, to abide in the Truth of I AM—remaining centered in I AM as our ALL in all.

Worship in its pure form is essentially recognizing our own utter dependency on God's ALL-ness while acknowledging God's infinite reality of being as our innermost consciousness. There are times of true worship when our mind simply cannot enter the presence of I AM. It is not capable of going to this infinite place. Mind chatter is completely out of place in the Presence of I AM.[7] There are times when our thinker must come to utter stillness in order for us to worship God in spirit and truth.

We will soon discover however, that it is not an easy task to bring to stillness a mind that is practiced in having unrestricted reign over its own thoughts. If you have ever tried to still your own anxious thoughts and quiet your own agitated emotions you will know how all pandemonium breaks loose when you call your soul to account. However, at such times we have the option to step over into our new identity in I AM and command our soul to *be still and know.* The Psalmist called his soul to account by voicing such sentiments as, "why are you cast down my soul, hope in God for I shall continually praise Him."[8]

The practice of consciously linking our breathing to the awareness of God's presence in us and around us can become a simple yet very powerful form of meditation where we acknowledge God in all our ways throughout the day. In this contemplation, we begin to realize that everything is spiritual, and as a result, we recognize the sacredness of each moment. It encourages us to sense the holiness that permeates everything. God is here—now! Wherever here and now are found, God is! God is nearer than near. Seeing the omnipresence of God in the moment *is* the way to God: "Whoever comes to God must believe that He *is.*"[9] Such sight can only arise from a birth of I AM within: "Except you are born from above you cannot see the kingdom of God."[10]

Pausing briefly at regular intervals to breathe in God and to breathe out our false self provides us the opportunity to give thanks in every situation. Such praise pauses can be initiated by almost any activity that we do on a regular basis. Simply linking the awareness of our breathing to habits like washing our hands or sitting down to a meal can awaken us into consciousness. For example, the routine act of brushing your teeth could be a reminder for you to pause and reflect on your breathing. A simple habit like brushing your teeth can serve to remind you to give thanks to God for sharing His breath with you. As your heart becomes practiced in gratefulness, you may be surprised to find yourself living in the awareness of God's infinite supply rather than in the conscious lack with which the mind so readily identifies in its own thoughts.

This doesn't mean we make a ritual of breathing or that we commit ourselves to breathing exercises at specific times and places. To do so may very well provide an opportunity for the mind to conquer reality again, locking it away inside mental constructs of religious ritual, separating us from life in the moment. Although we often imagine that we are the ones searching for reality, it does us good to be reminded that reality is not simply an unintelligent entity or an inert energy out there somewhere for which we are searching. Not at all! Reality is an infinite *person* searching for us. So whenever Reality knocks on the door of our thinking, we can respond immediately by becoming aware of our breathing within the infinite allness of Him with whom we are one.

Even if this awareness initially only lasts for a split second, it serves to awaken us into the Universal. As we thus practice the presence of Being, we will find ourselves awakening more and more into life—Life Himself rising up within us, giving us the light of a new day. This Ultimate Reality abides within, knocking on the door of our inner being, calling us to intimate conscious communion [11]—"We have therefore a more certain Prophetic Word [dwelling within] unto whom we do well to pay attention, as unto a lamp that shines in a dark place until the gentle day dawn when the Morning Star arises in your own hearts."[12] In this dawning of I AM within, we become increasingly conscious.

Stopping briefly to listen to the silence around us is another simple exercise that can assist in our awakening into the consciousness of Being. After identifying the audible sounds that envelop us, we can consciously step past the noise into the silence—into that space in which all sounds take place. It is this *space* which gives us the ability to distinguish all sounds. If there was no silence—only noise—we would not be able to hear anything. Identifying with this silence that surrounds and permeates everything can direct our attention to the infinite reality of God, much like becoming aware of our breath in the moment.

As we practice the awareness of breathing in the infinite depth of outer space, which is merely a reflection of that real universe of inner space called the kingdom of heaven, we may well find ourselves cooperating more and more with what God Himself is doing in us to bring us to that superconscious state of Himself as our life—fully knowing the indwelling presence of I AM within the all of God.

As we begin to awaken into the stereo consciousness we were created to walk in, we literally take the lid off our limitations. When our intellect is brought under the guidance of our intuition, we walk free in the kingdom of heaven. The ultimate potential of our humanity, once it is surrendered to our divinity, is not only enormous, but unlimited. The apostle Paul relates his human potential in these terms: "I can do *all* things *through Christ* who is my strength."[13] Once we wake up to the reality of universal Love, revealed in and through Christ Jesus in us as our true Self, we will realize that Love is truly the one and only power at work in the whole universe. When we identify with this power as our strength, as our I AM, we will discover that we are divinely empowered to accomplish anything and everything that is settled in heaven.

Once we realize that God and man are not two separate entities but fundamentally one, we step into that integrated stereo consciousness that incorporates the awareness of the created realm of material substance with the infinite reality of spirit being. Man was designed to walk in conscious union with God, i.e., in intimate relationship and fellowship with Love. As human beings, we are birthed out of the Divine Being, to live in conscious union with Deity—our humanity fused with holy divinity. This is our glory, our ultimate potential as created beings. In this glory, we do not lose our individuality but rather our individual personalities realize their full potential. Such glory is God's original and ultimate purpose for the human race!

It's time to wake up, take off our nightclothes of separation thinking (our old identity of independence), and get dressed up in our new identity as body members of Christ Himself: "For you are dead and your own life is hidden with Christ in God, so that when *Christ who is your life* appears, you also appear in union with Him, glorified!"[14] There are far too many of us who are sleepwalking, still walking around naked in our humanity, merely dreaming that we are awake in the real world. It is high time we get decent:

- "For this reason He says, 'Awake you who sleep and arise from the dead and Christ shall be your Light.'"[15]
- "Awake to righteousness, and do not sin [do not miss I AM], for some have no knowledge of Deity [for some hold to an ignorance of divinity]."[16]
- "So then let us not sleep, as others do, but let us stay awake and be observant."[17]

Truly we are being awakened into God—into His infinite presence in the midst of all. In the presence and through the power of His Holy Spirit who is ceaselessly at work within us and around us, we are becoming conscious of being one with the One: "You who were at one time alienated and enemies *in your mind* . . . now have been reconciled to [made one with] God by the death of His Son."[18] By the finished work of Jesus the Christ (our universal I AM manifested in human form), we are awakening into the consciousness of who we really are. There is no separation! "Death is swallowed up in victory!"[19] Through His death and resurrection in our hearts, as our I AM, we are learning to walk in the power and authority of our true Self. Only our I AM can tell us who we are, "As He *is* so are we *in this world*."[20]

Like our Father in heaven, we are beginning to *be*, true sons and daughters, fully privileged citizens in the kingdom of heaven! We are who our Father has made us! I AM and the Father are one! Through I AM, we have been given a birthright, which empowers us to say, "YES, I AM!"

"Arise and shine, for your Light has come and the glory of the I AM has risen within you!"[21]

Welcome to the real world!

Notes

1   Col. 1:16,17, italics added
2   Acts 17:28, italics added
3   John 17:21, emphasis added
4   John 17:3
5   John 6:53, 57
6   1 Cor. 6:17, paraphrase
7   Ps. 46:10
8   Ps. 42:5
9   Heb. 11:6, italics added
10 John 3:3
11 Rev. 3:20
12 2 Pet. 1:19
13 Phil. 4:13, italics added
14 Col. 3:3, italics added
15 Eph. 5:14
16 1 Cor. 15:34, paraphrase
17 1 Thess. 5:6
18 Col. 1:21,22, italics added
19 1 Cor. 15:54b
20 1 John 4:17b, italics added
21 Isa. 60:1, paraphrase

———

Yes, I AM

I am the place I AM shines through

I AM and I are ONE—not two!

I need not fear nor fret nor plan

My place is Now and as I AM

When I just BE, relaxed and free,

I AM then works His plan through me.

Glossary

carnal soul: The soul that is dependent upon the input of the five bodily senses (sight, hearing, touch, smell, and taste) for its identity; the soul that is spiritually dead—unable to detect or interact with spirit due to the insensibility of its inner organs of perception.

conscience: the human faculty of coperception, the inner ability to perceive in union with our inmost Being.

consciousness: The state of awareness that arises out of our innermost Being, independent of rational thought, the root of awareness that stands observant behind our thoughts.

human spirit: That inward faculty of the soul known as the heart, which mirrors the outward faculties of seeing, hearing, feeling, tasting, and smelling, sometimes referred to as intuition; that faculty of our human soul that interfaces with spirit.

identity: Our individual sense of self, determined by what and who we are identified with, either inwardly or outwardly.

Knower: The Discerner, the True Self, the Universal I AM, the Logos of God, the Holy Spirit of Christ within, the core consciousness of every human, the Ultimate Observer behind all thought.

Presence: The universal, infinite being of God, as well as the awakening realization of the infinite nature of God's universal being in the midst.

regenerated soul: The soul that has been reborn (regenerated) from the Center, the soul in which the Seed of Life has germinated, bringing resurrection to the dead faculties of the heart and rejuvenation to the outward senses of the thinker, deriving its identity from the indwelling presence of I AM.

repentance: The change of mind brought about in the soul when God interrupts the course of man's life causing him to reconsider his perception of reality.

soul: The double-faced faculty of our humanity that stands between heaven and earth constituting our unique individual personality (refer to chapter 2). The soul is the seat of the human will, the rational intellect and the natural affections (emotions), as well as the root of our intuition and conscience, which is also referred to as the heart of man or the human spirit.

spirit: The dimensionless reality of God; the permanent, unchanging, invisible (inwardly visible), universal reality of God's being.

stereo consciousness: The state of consciousness where the two faces of the soul operate in conscious union with spirit integrating the outer universe of materiality with the inward universe of spirit reality, a blended awareness of two cosmic realms, physical and spiritual.

thinker: The integrated faculties of the soul (intellect, emotions, and will) directed by the sensory perceptions of the body's senses of sight, taste, hearing, touch, and smell; a soul dependent on the flesh.

unconsciousness: The state of being unaware of the inward dimension of spirit, inward blindness to reality, an awareness totally dependent on sensory input from the outward sensory organs of perception.

veil: The inner blindness resulting from the spiritual death of the soul, the death shroud that consciously separates the thinker from the Knower; the unconscious state of the soul in relation to the indwelling spirit.

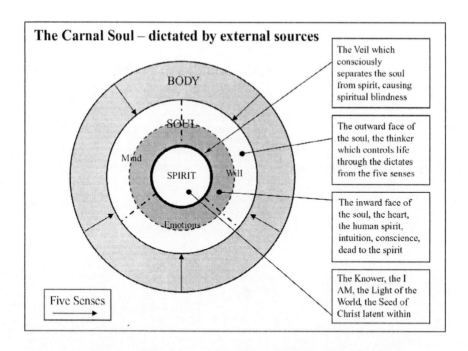

The Carnal Soul – dictated by external sources

BODY

SOUL

Mind

SPIRIT

Will

Emotions

Five Senses

The Veil which consciously separates the soul from spirit, causing spiritual blindness

The outward face of the soul, the thinker which controls life through the dictates from the five senses

The inward face of the soul, the heart, the human spirit, intuition, conscience, dead to the spirit

The Knower, the I AM, the Light of the World, the Seed of Christ latent within

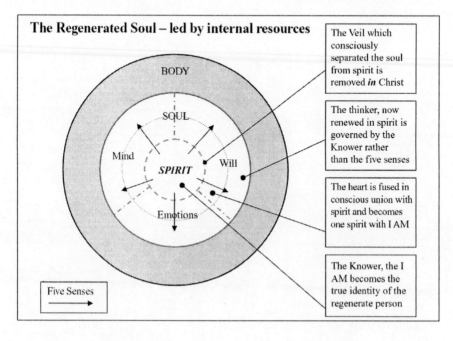

The Regenerated Soul – led by internal resources

BODY

SOUL

Mind

SPIRIT

Will

Emotions

Five Senses

The Veil which consciously separated the soul from spirit is removed *in* Christ

The thinker, now renewed in spirit is governed by the Knower rather than the five senses

The heart is fused in conscious union with spirit and becomes one spirit with I AM

The Knower, the I AM becomes the true identity of the regenerate person

Index

Edwards Brothers,Inc!
Thorofare, NJ 08086
22 July, 2010
BA2010203